T0127103

La rettorica

SECULAR COMMENTARY SERIES

GENERAL EDITORS
Robert R. Edwards
Michael J. Livingston

ADVISORY BOARD
Rita Copeland, *University of Pennsylvania*
John V. Fleming, *Princeton University*
William J. Kennedy, *Cornell University*
Alastair J. Minnis, *Yale University*
Richard J. Tarrant, *Harvard University*

The Secular Commentary Series provides modern English translations of medieval texts that analyze, annotate, and explicate classical and vernacular works. These texts date from the fourth through the sixteenth centuries, and they represent various traditions (grammatical, allegorical, exegetical, academic, and humanistic). The works they elucidate include poetry, fiction, history, philosophy, and scientific treatises. Each volume in the series contains a critical introduction and select bibliography, a clear prose translation, and notes designed to gloss difficult passages. The aim of the series is to support teaching in the broadest sense: the volumes are suitable for the classroom and serve as an aid to scholars and generalist readers across the full range of the humanities.

Medieval Institute Publications is a program of
The Medieval Institute, College of Arts and Sciences

 WESTERN MICHIGAN UNIVERSITY

Brunetto Latini
La rettorica

Edited and translated by
Stefania D'Agata D'Ottavi

TEAMS • Secular Commentary Series

MEDIEVAL INSTITUTE PUBLICATIONS
Western Michigan University
Kalamazoo

Copyright © 2016 by the Board of Trustees of Western Michigan University
All rights reserved

Library of Congress Cataloging-in-Publication Data

Latini, Brunetto, 1220-1295, author.
 [Rettorica. English]
 La rettorica / Brunetto Latini ; edited and translated by Stefania d'Agata
d'Ottavi.
     pages cm -- (TEAMS secular commentary series)
 Includes Cicero's De inventione and Latini's commentary.
 ISBN 978-1-58044-209-1 (paperbound : alk. paper)
 1. Rhetoric, Ancient--Early works to 1800. 2. Cicero, Marcus Tullius.
De inventione. I. D'Agata D'Ottavi, Stefania. II. Cicero, Marcus Tullius.
De inventione. 2016. III. Title. IV. Series: TEAMS secular commentary
series.
 PN185.L313 2016
 808.009'02--dc23
                                                        2015030960

Printed and bound in the United States of America.

Contents

Abbreviations

Beltrami

    Brunetto Latini. *Tresor*. Edited by Pietro G. Beltrami. Turin: Einaudi, 2007.

PL

    J.-P. Migne, ed. *Patrologiae cursus completus*, Series Latina. 221 vols. Paris: Migne, 1844–64.

RLM

    Karl Halm, ed. *Rhetores Latini minores*. Leipzig: B. G. Teubner, 1863. Reprint, Frankfurt am Main: Minerva, 1964.

Introduction

BRUNETTO LATINI'S *La rettorica* is the first Italian translation of Cicero's early and widely influential work *De inventione*. Medieval readers called the *De inventione* "the old rhetoric" (*rhetorica vetus*) and paired it with the pseudo-Ciceronian *Rhetorica ad Herennium*, "the new rhetoric" (*rhetorica nova*), to form the foundational texts of rhetorical theory before the fifteenth century.[1] Brunetto's *Rettorica* translates the first sixteen chapters of book 1 of the *De inventione* and part of the seventeenth (up to 17.1.24). It thus presents Cicero's civic framing of rhetoric and his teaching on the kinds and parts of rhetoric, the issues it addresses, the parts of an oration, and the ways of adapting the opening part of a speech (exordium) to different cases. Brunetto interrupts his translation, however, whenever he thinks commentary is needed. His commentary takes several forms—a paraphrase or restatement of doctrine, additional information needed for understanding or clarity, or a detailed gloss. At times Brunetto translates Cicero's text closely for four or five lines of prose, followed by an analysis that is much longer than the translated original. When he thinks that one aspect of Cicero's treatise is of outstanding importance, he turns to a detailed, more analytical examination of the text, and his comment looks like what has been called a *catena* gloss—that is, Brunetto quotes one or two words from Cicero's text and gives his own interpretation in an attempt to disclose Cicero's intention and to show that it is well suited to his purpose.[2] Brunetto divides his treatment of the text into 105 sections of translation and commentary. The commentary is usually not word-by-word because Brunetto is more interested in showing how the classical ideas on rhetoric can suit the requirements of the communal civilization than in offering an academic *lectio* of Cicero.

The beginning of the literary history of Italy coincides with the establishment of the commune and with the birth of the new social classes of politicians and merchants.[3] Among them ancient culture and Latin tradition were held in great esteem, since these provided legitimization for the new classes of rulers and intellectuals. According to Brunetto (1.16), Rome is the "comune d'ogne uomo" (every man's commune). Roman history was a model to be studied and imitated in order to achieve the greatness that Rome had enjoyed for so many centuries. It was therefore important to find a relationship between Roman civilization and the political and social features of the Florentine commune in order to establish it as the best possible form of government. No surprise, then, that in his *Rettorica* Brunetto constantly translates Cicero's Latin *res publica* by Italian *commune*. The characters of Caesar, Cato, and Catiline are likewise discussed in *La rettorica* as if they were Brunetto's contemporaries. This must have been a very well known practice, for, in a different context, Dino Compagni compares his political and personal enemy, Corso Donati, to Catiline.[4]

The translation of Latin works into the vernacular became the main vehicle through which to restore this reborn vision of classical culture, and, at least at the beginning, translation served chiefly practical purposes—to teach how to speak well in public and to write letters in an appropriate language. This is no doubt why in *La rettorica* Brunetto is so anxious to give the rules of the *ars dictaminis* (the art of letter writing) the same status traditionally held by the rules of rhetoric. At the same time, he applies both rhetorical genres to suit the requirements of the city-state and the Florentine commune in particular. From this point of view, the works of Cicero offered an example of republican ideals, of rhetorical doctrine, and of exemplary prose.

Brunetto Latini

Brunetto was known to his contemporaries as a philosopher, notary, rhetorician, epistolographer, and politician. In his *Nuova cronica* (9.10), a history of Florence from its mythological origins through the Black Death and beyond, Giovanni Villani describes Brunetto as a

> gran filosofo e . . . sommo maestro in rettorica, tanto in bene sapere dire come in bene dittare . . . egli fu tanto cominciatore e maestro in digrossare i Fiorentini e farli scorti di bene parlare, e in saper guidare e reggere la nostra repubblica secondo la politica.

> (a great philosopher and an outstanding master of rhetoric, excellent both in oratory and in letter writing. He was initiator and master of the art of refining the Florentines and of making them proficient both in speaking well and in guiding and ruling our republic according to the laws of politics.)

As Francesco Mazzoni suggests, Brunetto was a teaching master for the city of Florence.[5] He put rhetoric at the service of good government, and he showed how Latin and French cultures could suit the development of the Florentine city-republic. He did so first of all by translating Cicero not only to make his writings accessible to a wider audience but also to stress that Cicero's civic passion, which had induced him to put rhetoric at the service of politics, was also his own. This is the real heritage Brunetto left to the Florentines, and in this sense it is true that he was Dante's master, although the poet's conclusions were ultimately to be very different from the notary's teachings.[6]

Brunetto's role as a master of Florentine civic life may lie behind the role for which he is better known—Dante's teacher and master. In the third circle of *Inferno*, where Dante meets people who have been violent against God, nature, or art, the poet addresses Brunetto as "La cara buona imagine paterna / di voi quando nel mondo ad ora ad ora / m'insegnavate come l'uom s'etterna" (the dear kindly paternal image of you who when in the world whenever the opportunity presented itself taught me how man can make himself eternal) (15.83–85). These lines, together with the place Dante gives Brunetto in Hell, among the sodomites, have long puzzled scholars. No exact record of Dante as Brunetto's pupil exists, although the connection is often mentioned in the commentaries from the mid-fourteenth century onward, and must soon have become an established tradition, nor is Brunetto known to have held any official position as a teacher. Villani (*Nuova cronica* 9.10) qualifies his praise of Brunetto by remarking that he is a "mondano uomo" (dissolute man).[7] Brunetto confesses earlier in the *Tesoretto* that he is among those considered "un poco mondanetto" (a little dissolute) (line 2561). How close dissolution comes to meaning sodomy is unclear. For his part, Brunetto declares sodomy the worst form of lechery (*Tesoretto*, lines 2859–61).

Brunetto was born in Florence around 1220 to Ser Bonaccorso Latini della Lastra, a judge and a notary. The family name is sometimes spelled "Latini," in the genitive, after the Tuscan fashion, and sometimes "Latino." Brunetto's given name is spelled as "Brunetto" or "Burnetto/Burnecto" in a common metathesis. Latin documents are signed "Burnectus Latinus." In remarkable ways, the story of his life is closely related to the history of Florence itself. He may have studied law at the University of Bologna, but it was in Florence that his career began and developed.[8] Its first phase, approximately from 1250 to 1260, coincided with the new democratic constitution adopted by the Florentines shortly after Frederick

II's death in 1250. The Signoria was formed by the Capitano del Popolo and twelve counselors, two for each *sesto*, the parts into which the city was divided. These were the Elders (*Gli Anziani*): they formed a council where every decision concerning all the aspects, both civil and military, of the city life was taken. When Frederick II died, the Guelphs returned to Florence, and a Guelph *podestà* (city administrator) was elected. These officers, whose task was to see that the law was respected and obeyed, usually came from other cities (the first came from Milan) and held office for six months or one year, after which another *podestà* was appointed. From 1250 to 1254, peace treaties were signed with Pistoia, Siena, and even Pisa, a traditional enemy of Florence. We find Brunetto's name for the first time in 1254 as a notary and scribe for the commune, on behalf of which he prepared and signed several documents between March 31 and April 6. On April 20 he prepared and signed the text of the important peace treaty with Siena. On October 10 of the same year Brunetto acted as a public speaker in the arbitration of Florence between Genoa and Pisa; on this occasion, Brunetto is called "chancellor" of the Florentine Commune.[9]

In 1258 the Ghibellines, protected by Frederick II's successor, Manfred, organized various plots against the city of Florence, and consequently they were banished from the city; many of their supporters, mostly members of the Uberti family, were killed. The abbot of Vallombrosa, of the noble family of the Beccheria, was accused, perhaps unjustly, of having sided with the Ghibellines and was murdered. The pope reacted immediately to the murder with an interdict against Florence, and the Florentine council of the Elders was forced to reply with an official letter that Brunetto may have composed.[10] The Ghibelline refugees, helped by King Manfred, gathered in Siena and were planning war against Florence. *Il Libro di Montaperti* (*The Book of Montaperti*) mentions Brunetto as *sindaco* (counselor) of Montevarchi, a town near Florence.

In 1260 the Commune of Florence sent Brunetto to Alfonso of Castille (El Sabio) in order to persuade him to claim the imperial crown against Manfred, while Guglielmo Beroardi was sent to Richard of Cornwall with the same purpose. In this way the Florentine republic tried to oppose the Ghibellines, who had Manfred's support. But all was in vain: on September 4, 1260 the Florentines were defeated by the Sienese at Montaperti. This ended the government of what has been called the *primo popolo* which had ruled over Florence for ten years. In his *Tesoretto* (lines 135–62), Brunetto relates these important historical events to his personal story. He says that he was on his way back from Spain when in the plain of Roncesvalles (associated with the French epic hero Roland and the traitor Ganelon) he met a student who informed him of the Guelph defeat at Montaperti as well as of the fact that the faction to which he belonged had been banished from Florence. A letter, probably written by Brunetto's father, Bonaccorso, mentions the same facts.[11] In any case, it was clearly dangerous for him to go back to his city. Brunetto therefore stopped in France, where he found a friend, perhaps one of the Tosinghi family, whom in *La rettorica* he calls his "harbor". This friend greatly helped Brunetto, and Brunetto's major works are dedicated to him. We know Brunetto spent time at Arras, Bar-sur-Aube, Montpellier, and Paris, where as a notary he signed documents for some Florentine merchants. It was almost certainly in France that Brunetto composed his most important works—*La rettorica, Li livres dou Tresor* (*Tresor*), *Tesoretto, Favolello*—some poetry, and probably the translations of Cicero's three so-called Caesarian orations (*Pro Marcello, Pro Ligario,* and *Pro rege Deiotaro*).

The historical events that followed the episode of Montaperti are as complex and intricate as the ones that preceded it. In 1265 Charles of Anjou was called by the Florentine government to help the Guelphs, and Brunetto may have returned to Florence as one of his followers.[12] After the Battle of Benevento (1266), the Ghibellines were forced to leave Florence, and the Guelphs were once more able to return. Charles of Anjou entered Florence on May 7, 1267 and was elected *podestà* for a period of seven years. A Guelph league was formed during the siege of the Ghibelline city of Poggibonsi, near Siena. On this occasion Brunetto was one of the king's notaries. For him it was the beginning of a second career, this time one of open political engagement. In 1268 Brunetto was a counselor of the king's delegates in Tuscany and *prothonotarius* (the head of the notaries) to one of them, Jean Britaud, who played an important part in the battle of Tagliacozzo. In 1272 Brunetto was Secretary of the Chancery, and in 1273 he was mentioned as *prothonotarius* of the Republic. In 1275 he was consul for the Guild of Judges and Notaries of his district.

In 1279 Pope Nicholas III attempted to establish a peace treaty between the conflicting parties, and Cardinal Latino Malabranca was entrusted with the mission. Brunetto Latini, along with Guido Cavalcanti, is known to have been in the Guelph committee that was to discuss the conditions of the peace. In 1282 the priorate, a government centered in the guilds, was established in Florence. On October 21 Brunetto spoke before the Council of the Capitano del Popolo in favor on a petition raised by the Guelph commanders. In 1284 he was a member of the council of the *podestà* with Dino Compagni and Guido Cavalcanti. In the same year, he prepared and signed with Manetto Benincasa a treaty between Florence, Lucca, and Genoa against Pisa, which had been recently defeated in the Battle of the Meloria. The document can be found in *Liber iurium reipublicae Genuensis*, and it may be the most important act in Brunetto's political life.[13] In spite of the verbal violence and the high-flown rhetoric of the text, however, the treaty had little political effect, since Florence always tried to avoid open hostilities.

On February 3, 1285 Brunetto spoke in the Consiglio dei Savi in favor of a prudent and moderate application of the treaty against Pisa, while before him Corso Donati had argued that no agreement should be sought with Count Ugolino della Gherardesca and that the strict terms of the treaty should be honored without hesitation. On March 17 of the same year, Brunetto spoke in the Consiglio Generale del Capitano to plead for a certain freedom of action for the ambassadors who had to decide the time of the assault against Pisa. His speech aimed at delaying action and attempting to reach an agreement in light of growing Ghibelline strength after the death of Charles of Anjou earlier in the year.

In 1287 Brunetto was appointed prior (one of twelve guild rectors and ruling magistrates of the Florentine republic) for the district of Porta a Duomo from August 15 to October 15. During those months he was in the Torre della Castagna, just in front of the house where Dante Alighieri (then twenty-two years old) lived. Thirteen years later the same Torre della Castagna would have Dante as its inmate in one of the stormiest periods of the Florentine political history.[14] The events following—Count Ugolino's betrayal and the preparation of the war against Arezzo—saw Brunetto as a speaker in various councils, generally in favor of the war against Pisa and the Ghibelline cities, especially after the victory of Florence at Campaldino in 1289. Brunetto was also involved in the problems concerning the organization of the Commune of Florence, as is shown by some of his speeches in 1290, 1291, and 1292. The last record of his public life is a speech before the Consiglio dei Savi on July 22, 1292.[15] Brunetto Latini died in 1293 and was buried in the church of Santa Maria Maggiore.[16]

The Works of Brunetto Latini

Apart from the documents he prepared and signed for the Florentine commune and for private parties (e.g., merchants he met in France), Brunetto wrote all his extant works during his exile. *La rettorica*, *Tresor*, *Tesoretto*, *Favolello*, and some poetry were all written in France and show Brunetto's assimilation of the French culture of his time. Probably at about the same time, he also translated into the vernacular three famous orations by Cicero—*Pro Ligario*, *Pro Marcello*, and *Pro rege Deiotaro*.

Tresor was written in French. Brunetto explains that he chose to write in French first because he happened to be in France, and second because the French language is "plus delitable et plus commune à tous langages" (1.1.7). French was, in fact, recognized as an international language, and *Tresor* aimed at an international audience. When Brunetto wrote it, he had already started *La rettorica* and perhaps the three orations. The Italian *volgare* was therefore recognized as a proper vehicle for lofty ideas and discourse. But *La rettorica*, as we have seen, aims at teaching the use of this art in political matters and is specially, if indirectly, concerned with the intricate events of the Florentine city-state. *Tresor*, by contrast, is an encyclopedia, and its relationship to the actual government of a city-state is, at least theoretically, much looser than in *La rettorica*. The third book of *Tresor* includes very detailed rules for the practice of good government, but this is part of the much more general outlook of this work. Therefore, it is appropriate that the language should be the one that was considered the most international.

Tresor is divided into three parts. The first is mainly theoretical and deals with the divisions of philosophy, the creation of the world, universal history, the natures of earthly things, the elements, the composition of the sky, and the various kinds of animals. The second book discusses ethics and its subdivisions as well as vices and virtues. It consists of a partial translation of Aristotle's *Nicomachean Ethics*. The third book concerns rhetoric and politics. If compared to other encyclopedic works of the time (especially Vincent of Beauvais's *Speculum maius*), which are often considered Brunetto's sources, *Tresor* clearly omits many subjects: there is, for example, no mention of arithmetic, geometry, or music. The fact is that Brunetto never really loses sight of his main interest, which is the civil life of cities. Despite his desire to be exhaustive, he tends to mention mainly those subjects that are capable of leading him more or less directly to his main concern. *Tresor* was immediately successful (more than a hundred manuscripts survive); it was translated into Castilian, Catalan, French, Latin, and Sicilian. A Tuscan version attributed, perhaps wrongly, to Bono Giamboni also exists. Brunetto's fame relied for centuries on it alone.

Il Tesoretto (*Little Treasure*) was also composed in France, but it is written in Italian in couplets of septenaries, according to the fashion of French poetry. It consists of 2944 lines and is unfinished. Brunetto's main source is

Alan de Lille's *De planctu naturae*, both in theme and structure. *Il Tesoretto* is an allegorical vision in which Nature, the cardinal virtues, the God of Love, and other traditional characters explain the principles of natural philosophy, describe vices and virtues, and discuss the seven liberal arts. This work shows how deeply Brunetto had assimilated French culture and the *Roman de la Rose*, especially the first part composed by Guillaume de Lorris.

Favolello (from the French *fablel*, "a little poem"), composed in response to a now-lost poem by Rustico di Filippo, is also written in Italian in couplets of septenaries. Brunetto's poem is a short treatise on friendship. It follows the well-known tradition of Cicero's *Laelius*, which had enjoyed a revival in the works of Aelred of Rielvaux, Bernard of Clairvaux, Andreas Capellanus, and the *Amicitia* by Boncompagno da Signa, which Brunetto probably knew very well.[17]

Scholars attribute to Brunetto Latini the canzone "S'eo son distretto innamoratamente" (If I Am Bound by the Chains of Love), which survives in only one manuscript (Vatican City, Biblioteca Apostolica Vaticana, MS Latino 3973). D'Arco Silvio Avalle interprets the song as a homosexual homage addressed to Bondie Dietaiuti who, according to this hypothesis, provided an answer in the song that follows Brunetto's poem in the manuscript, "Amor, quando mi membra " (Love, When I Remember). This exchange would explain the place that Dante gives Brunetto in the *Commedia*. The interpretation has been questioned by some scholars, according to whom Dante's condemnation is allegorical and related to what he had already indirectly reproached in his "master," that is, the fact of writing in a language not his own, which he considered against nature (*Convivio* 1.11).[18]

La rettorica

Brunetto probably wrote *La rettorica* in 1262, when he was in France and could not return to Florence from his mission to Spain because the city was in the hands of the Ghibellines. It was in France that he met the friend to whom his work is dedicated and whose identity is still unknown, in spite of many hypotheses. During this time his knowledge of French culture must have greatly improved, and Brunetto may have become interested in widening the field of his interests. His knowledge of French encyclopedias probably suggested the composition of a complex and wide-ranging work that aimed at covering all the branches of learning, such as *Tresor*. This is the usually accepted reason for his interrupting the translation of *La rettorica* partway through book 1 of the *De inventione*. (Book 3 of *Tresor* includes a somewhat modified version of *La rettorica*.) Alternatively,

Brunetto may have left *La rettorica* unfinished because his commentary on Cicero's text was growing out of all proportion and would have made the final text much too long.[19]

Brunetto begins *La rettorica* with the conventional modesty *topos*, in which a writer professes inability to address his or her subject matter. The strategy of *diminutio* extends to the actual layout of the page (a sort of *dispositio*). As Brunetto's title explains, the large letters on the page refer to the text of Cicero, while the smaller ones refer to the Commentator's words. One of the most reliable manuscripts of *La rettorica*, Florence, Biblioteca Nazionale Centrale, Magliabechiano, II, IV, 127 (M[1]), presents this in the fourteenth-century scribe's interpretation where the parts translated from Cicero are written in slightly larger letters than Brunetto's commentary. In the majuscule "S" of the first word of the text (*Sovente*, "often") the rubric shows an image of Cicero (above) and Brunetto (below), thus expressing symbolically the superiority of the ancient master and the position of Brunetto as his pupil. In spite of the formal homage to Cicero, however, Brunetto considers his comment on the same level as the text he is translating; thus, while Cicero is "the wisest among the Romans" (1.7), Brunetto

> put all his passion and learning into explaining and clarifying what Tullius had said. This is the person this book refers to as "the Commentator," [*lo Sponitore*] that is, the one who expounds and illustrates Tullius's book, both in his own words and in those of the ancient philosophers and masters, and as much more as is needed by the art of what was neglected in Tullius's book, as the careful reader will find in what follows. (1.7).

This is why Brunetto says that the work has two authors (1.7), and he establishes a constant dialogue with Cicero's text in order to be able to apply the principles of rhetoric to other genres of discourse, such as letter writing, which is generally considered his most original contribution to the work.

An important sign of Brunetto's intention of "collaborating" with Cicero in explaining and using the art of rhetoric for his own purposes can be found in the prologue, which consists of two parts: the first concerns the definition of rhetoric and is the formulation given by Cicero; the second appears to be a prologue to Brunetto's own comment and shows how seriously Brunetto's view of himself as a second author must be taken.

> This work has two authors: one who composed his book on rhetoric both out of the precepts of all the philosophers who lived before

him and from the vivid source of his own mind, that is, Marcus
Tullius Cicero, the wisest among the Romans. The second is Brunetto Latino, Florentine, who put all his passion and learning into
explaining and clarifying what Tullius had said. This is the person
this book refers to as "the Commentator," that is, the one who
expounds and illustrates Tullius's book, both in his own words and
in those of the ancient philosophers and masters, and as much more
as is needed by the art of what was neglected in Tullius's book, as the
careful reader will find in what follows. (1.7)

Brunetto's prologue is in the tradition of the medieval *Accessus ad auctores* in terms of its structure and method of classification: the author,
the intention, the subject matter, the form, the motive, the usefulness,
and the title are duly given in the usual sequence.[20] In this way Brunetto
shows his ambition to be considered the Cicero of his time. Describing
Cicero as a *homo novus*, Brunetto emphasizes that his political outlook
was republican: his struggle against Catiline, a nobleman, and his siding
with Pompey in the civil war showed that he belonged to that emerging
class of people who had reached important positions because of their
abilities and not their birth. Accordingly, Brunetto himself was also a
homo novus, not because of his birth but because of his profession of
notarius and *dictator*, a profession that was gaining increasing importance in the affairs of the city-states and that placed him at the very
center of important political and diplomatic dealings.[21]

The title *La rettorica* is spelled in all extant manuscripts with a double
t: in the first vernacular translation of Latin texts, the word was believed to
derive from *rector* (ruler) rather than *rhetor* (teacher of oratory or rhetorician). This probably has something to do with the fact that both the rendering of Latin rhetorical works into Italian and the revival of Ciceronian rhetoric are closely related to the birth of the city-states and to the rise of Italian
communal culture. The etymology is meant to emphasize that a good ruler
is also a wise and competent speaker. The quality of *sapientia* (wisdom) is
essential to the good orator, and its importance is stressed throughout the
book and in all medieval commentaries on *De inventione*. A wise *rhetor/
rector* is of the utmost importance if rhetoric is to be useful to political
life: people who can speak well but have no wisdom are dangerous to the
community to which they belong. Thierry of Chartres, the twelfth-century
commentator on the *De inventione* and *Rhetorica ad Herennium*, maintains
that the civil function of rhetoric is possible only if a close relationship
exists between rhetoric and wisdom. In the medieval schools the teaching of

rhetoric was related to ethics.[22] The art of eloquence was considered useful to politics and capable of solving conflicts, which within and among the city-states were frequent and fierce, only if joined to wisdom. In order to emphasize the importance of wisdom, Brunetto traces the origin of rhetoric back to the birth of civilization. From their previous wild condition, men, who used to live like animals, were ultimately persuaded by a wise man to live according to rules, and this decision gave rise to cities and societies. This wise man had understood the potentialities of mankind and encouraged people to gather together, to live under the same laws and according to the same principles of ethics and politics. This is what is called a civilized society, the best of which is a well ruled republic, a city-state where the *rector* achieves the best results if he is also a wise *rhetor*. At its birth rhetoric seemed therefore to have something of the process of creation. It was able to give shape and order to a shapeless world and to bring man to live according to his true nature, which in Aristotle's definition is that of a social and political animal, a quality that is best displayed in the rational use of language.[23] Since language is what distinguishes men from animals, it follows that the one who has acquired language in the highest degree is also the best possible ruler: in repeating some of the most famous Aristotelian concepts, Brunetto expresses himself in the language of logic and comes close to forming syllogisms, for example, when he discusses the superiority of man over animals as far as the possession of language is concerned (15.1).

One of the most compelling symbols of the achievement of virtue through eloquence is the figure of Ulysses, who is often mentioned by Brunetto as a wise and virtuous man. Giuseppe Mazzotta analyzes Dante's portrayal of Ulysses in the *Commedia* in light of Ciceronian rhetoric and its interpretation by Brunetto. Mazzotta shows the verbal and conceptual analogies between the episode of Ulysses in *Inferno* 26 and Cicero's and Brunetto's ideas of language and of rhetoric.[24] When Ulysses' men have recovered their human shapes after Circe's spell had transformed them into animals, Ulysses indicates to them where he thinks virtue and knowledge lie. Moreover, Mazzotta remarks that the whole Odyssey was considered by Neoplatonic thinkers to be an allegory of education. Dante, however, goes further and develops a much more skeptical attitude toward the relationship between virtue and rhetoric and toward the power of language in general. His Ulysses, after all, fails and is lost with his companions, but Dante looks to Cicero and Brunetto to show the ideas he will ultimately re-elaborate and reinterpret.

The urgency to find a place for rhetoric among the other sciences leads Brunetto to a detailed classification of human knowledge, which anticipates the more complex treatment he was to develop in *Tresor*. Rhetoric is considered essential to mankind not just as one of the liberal arts but as a philosophical discipline. As such, it is surely part of the thinking process and cannot be neglected. Starting with philosophy, the *scientia scientiarum*, which he divides into practice, logic, and metaphysics, Brunetto classifies all human knowledge in a series of diagram trees that illustrate the taxonomic interest he was developing. When he comes to politics, he explains that it can be practiced "by deeds" or "by words" (17.17). Both subdivisions are interesting. "Deeds" refers to the arts and crafts that played such an important part in the city-states, not only in the life of people in general but also in the government of the city, since belonging to one of the guilds was an essential requisite to taking part in the city's political life. Politics "by words" is that which "can be obtained by language alone," and its subdivisions are grammar, dialectics, and rhetoric, that is, the arts of the *trivium*, the foundational areas of the seven liberal arts.

In making his classification more complex, Brunetto gives rhetoric, as it were, a noble descent, since he derives it from philosophy and claims it to be on equal footing with the other sciences. This idea is not completely original: in the thirteenth century Aristotle's works were beginning to be known much better than before thanks to the translations by Arabic and European scholars, who had by then more reliable texts at their disposal. In particular, *Nicomachean Ethics*, where a similar classification can be found, had been translated into Latin by Hermann the German, an edition Brunetto probably knew; although in the second book of *Tresor*, he says that he translated Aristotle's *Ethics* himself.[25] In any case, what is important is the connection that Brunetto establishes between the well-known arts of the *trivium* and politics, between politics and logic, and ultimately with philosophy. This allows him to explain Cicero's indication of the subject matter of rhetoric (demonstration, deliberation, and judgment) by means of logical demonstrations and to justify his refusal of Hermagoras's theory in a series of syllogisms. Hermagoras maintained that because rhetoric is part of philosophy, it can concern the same questions that are dealt with by that science. But what interests Cicero and, above all, Brunetto is the fact that rather than consisting of disagreement about general matters, rhetoric concerns contention about specific points (25.6).

Once Brunetto has given rhetoric its proper place among the sciences, he can proceed to analyze its parts according to the usual fivefold division: *inventio* (the discovery of topics), *dispositio* (arrangement), *elocutio* (style), *memoria* (memory), and *pronuntiatio* (delivery). He is anxious to emphasize that the kinds of controversies where rhetoric is essential are not only those that are dealt with in law courts but mainly those that arise within a city and with other city-states. Brunetto's experience as a notary and his negotiations with allies and enemies of Florence must have taught him that a good orator had an important task in diplomacy and politics. From this point of view, the so-called *constitutio generalis* (general issue) is of special interest and Brunetto comments on Cicero's words:

> trials are best dealt with by jurists, while rhetoric shows how to speak appropriately on a certain case which is not necessarily to be tried in court, nor always to occur between an accuser and an accused, but concerns other matters as well, such as the correct language in diplomatic missions, in councils of lords and of Communes, as well as the style of a well-composed letter. (76.4)

The examples Brunetto gives in this part of his comment are perfectly consistent with the ideas expressed above: they are all drawn from the often antagonistic relationship between city-states, and when he cannot easily apply the ones given by Cicero to what interests him, he modifies the examples, modernizes, and even invents them. Brunetto alternatively gives examples taken from ancient mythology (the stories of Ulysses and Ajax, Clytemnestra and Orestes, and Medea and her children), from the history of Rome (the enmity between Cato and Catiline, the speech of Pompey to his army), and from episodes of the world in which he was living. A lively society of Florentine merchants and craftsmen, Venetian and Genoese sailors, and, generally speaking, all the representatives of the communal middle class gives us a glimpse of what legal debates must have been like at the time Brunetto was writing, while the tasks of the various counselors and government officers are represented with great immediacy. The examples imply once more that the Florentine commune was the direct heir of the glory and the power of ancient Rome.[26]

Once the detailed classification of legal cases has been completed, Brunetto turns to the *ars dictaminis* and skilfully refers all he has said about oratory to the art of letter writing. Here Brunetto deals with a potentially serious contradiction to his theory. Cicero recognizes that conflict is the actual material of rhetoric, while some letters seem by their nature incompatible with the idea of conflict: how can a love letter, for example, be considered a document of contention? And if there are aspects of *ars dictaminis* that do not involve contrast, there can be only two solutions to the problem of its relationship with rhetoric: either the art of letter writing has different rules with respect to oratory, or it must be admitted that eloquence has a wider field than merely controversial matters. The latter option was Hermagoras's opinion, which both Cicero and Brunetto rejected.

Brunetto's solution to the problem is twofold. He first extends the concept of controversy:

> If the natures of a letter or of a song are carefully considered, it is easy to see that whoever composes a poem or sends a letter wishes to obtain something from the addressee, and this can be done by pleading, asking, ordering, threatening, comforting, or advising, and the same applies to the receiver of the letter, who can defend himself or refuse what he is asked by the same means. (76.16)[27]

The same rules, although with some differences, can apply to oratory as well as to letter writing, and because these are essentially of the same nature, their features can be analyzed with the same logical methods, and they ultimately lead to the same results. Then, Brunetto considers some differences between orations and letters and admits that his opinion differs from that of Cicero on some points, but he tries to minimize the differences by establishing all the possible similarities between the art of rhetoric and epistolography:

> It is easy to understand that these can also be the parts of a letter, whatever its subject. Three parts, namely exordium, narration, and conclusion, are equally suitable to an oration and to a letter; the other three, namely partition, confirmation, and refutation, are either less important in a letter or altogether absent. (76.25)

Some parts are common to both, while others are typical of one of the two kinds of expression. Once Brunetto has secured for *ars dictaminis* a place in contemporary culture comparable to that of eloquence, he can proceed to describe the differences and to emphasize the importance of an aspect that is not present in classical oratory, the initial greeting (*la salutazione*), which he calls the "gate" to the letter (*porta della pistola*):

> I claim, however, that the salutation is the gate, as it were, of the letter, in that it gives people's names and qualifications clearly. . . . It is therefore evident that the salutation is as part of a letter as the eye

is part of a man's body, and just as the eye is a noble part of man's
body, so is the salutation a noble part of the letter, since it gives light
to it, as the eye lights up a man's face. (76.27–28)

Brunetto then gives a minute classification of individual cases: there are
rules to be followed when writing to one's superiors or to one's inferiors,
and the social ranks of addresser and addressee are shown to be relevant to
the style and the content of the letter. Apart from these differences, oratory
and letter writing have the same dignity and can henceforth be considered
together, since they are both based on some kind of controversy. Adversarial rhetoric, whether in orations or in letter writing, is extended to political
discourse, in complete agreement with the situation of thirteenth-century
Italy. Little by little, therefore, the analysis comes once more to be centered
on eloquence: there are cases where there is no salutation in a letter, others
when it is replaced by some other forms of greeting and of endearment;
above all, when we write, we should imagine how we would behave if we
were in the presence of our addressee. The issue thus becomes the way in
which our attitude toward various kinds of people can be reproduced in
the language of the letter. Moreover, if we recall that letters were generally
read aloud, the matter comes full circle, and we understand why Brunetto
argues for the similarity of oratory and letter writing so strongly.

The remainder of Brunetto's discussion deals with the exordium, the
opening portion of a discourse that announces its subject and purpose and
tries to secure the goodwill of addressees. Brunetto's discussion applies to
orations and to letters alike, since it concerns the ways to persuade audiences. The translation and consequently the comment are interrupted at
this point (104.6; *De inventione* 1.24). It is impossible to imagine whether
more differences between eloquence and *dictamen* would have been found
had the discussion proceeded to analyze the other parts of the oration. In
Tresor, which was written after *La rettorica*, in spite of some statements
concerning the difference between these two genera of eloquence, *ars dictaminis* and oratory are dealt with together. But in this later work the focus
lies elsewhere, in a systemization and encyclopedic approach to knowledge.

La rettorica is the first treatise in the Italian vernacular to legitimize
the political use of rhetoric and give *dictamen* not only the practical importance it had had for a long time but also the theoretical and philosophical
basis that had hitherto been limited to the discussion of forensic oratory
alone. Brunetto firmly believes that the Ciceronian outlook can provide
an exemplary model for politics and especially for the politics that the

Florentine city-republic was developing in the later thirteenth century. By implying that Florence was the true heir of the republican ideals of ancient Rome, Brunetto shows that he believes in a sort of universal and immutable history that can manifest itself whenever the suitable conditions arise. His outlook is, from this point of view, entirely medieval.[28] Moreover, he is not interested in studying Ciceronian rhetoric as a revival of classic culture, nor is he looking for a philological reconstruction of Cicero's text, as Humanism and the Renaissance will do, because of their different ideas about classical antiquity, translation, and the integrity of a text. Brunetto is very much a man of his own time, and the importance of his work lies in the relationship he establishes between ancient rhetorical theory and modern political events.[29]

The language of *La rettorica* has neither the originality of Dante nor the elegance of Guittone d'Arezzo. It is, however, one of the first examples of the vernacular that does not try to imitate the forms and the style of Latin, but tries instead to create a style comparable to the clarity and the elegance of the Latin prose. A well-balanced and clear prose seems to be Brunetto's ideal. He does not use the intricate *ornatus* (adornment) and the excess of figures of other writers, such as the Bolognese authority on *dictamen* Guido Faba, but remains closer to the popular narrative style of his time. Coordination prevails over subordination in forms such as *et anche* (and also) and *e così* (and so). In thirteenth-century Italy these forms are typical of a kind of writing that aims at reaching less-cultured readers.[30] Repetitions and parataxis show the writer's constant search for clarity and his attempt to find (or create) the vernacular equivalent of important Latin expressions. Moreover, Brunetto's prose is greatly influenced by the necessity to explain Cicero's ideas as well as his own, and I would like to suggest that the style of his commentary is not too different from that of his translation, both because he needs unity and consistency in his prose and because his attitude is that of a teacher who needs a clear text to explain in clear glosses. One more feature should be emphasized. Brunetto's explanatory style is perfectly consistent with the fact that, in the academic circles he must have attended, rhetoric was part of logic. Therefore, expressions that highlight the logical consequences of an idea suit the requirements both of expounding Cicero's doctrine and of acknowledging the place the discipline had in university *curricula*. In spite of the admiration he always shows when dealing with Cicero's language, Brunetto is very careful not to create a too sharp contrast between the style of the translation and that of the commentary, since, as he himself says, his aim is to be the second author of the book. The clarity of the language and the logic of the exposition give the Tuscan vernacular Brunetto uses a new dignity and create the conditions for its more creative re-elaboration in Dante's *Convivio*.

Sources

Although *La rettorica* translates only a portion of the first book of the *De inventione*, the complete text of Cicero's treatise must be considered a source for Brunetto. He had probably planned a complete translation of the treatise, and it is evident that he knew it all. The examples he gives in his comments, for instance, are often drawn from the second book of *De inventione*, where Cicero himself finds examples to explain the theoretical issues he has been raising in the first part. While Brunetto often modifies the examples and changes the names of people and places in order to adjust them to the contemporary situation of Italy, and of Florence in particular, when he explains "Cicero with Cicero," he is at his best. In such cases, he fulfills his real aim, which is to show that Cicero is *the* authority when civic and republican ideals are at issue. The pseudo-Ciceronian *Rhetorica ad Herennium*, the "new rhetoric" that Guidotto da Bologna translated into Italian as *Fiore di rettorica*, is also a source for Brunetto, especially for some episodes (see, for example 2.22.34, where Medea is mentioned). The two translations appear together in several manuscripts of *La rettorica*. *De officiis* is also explicitly quoted by Brunetto when he states that faith is the foundation of justice (1.7.23 and 7.2), although some scholars question Brunetto's knowledge of the original text and believe he may have found the quotation in *Gli ammaestramenti degli antichi* (*The Teachings of the Ancients*) (dist. 15, cap. 1, par. 4), written by the Dominican friar and professor of philosophy Bartolomeo da San Concordio. *Pro Marcello* is often quoted when Caesar is praised, and it repeats some of the themes of the oration Brunetto translated.

Apart from Cicero, the fourth-century Commentator Gaius Marius Victorinus, who composed the earliest complete commentary on the *De inventione*, is a main source for Brunetto. Victorinus is interested in analyzing Cicero's rhetoric from a logical point of view and engages in endless demonstrations, often in the form of syllogisms, which Brunetto generally discards. The result is that Brunetto's prose is much more lively and agile than Victorinus's, and his focus is evidently a different one.[31] Victorinus serves Brunetto mainly as a source of examples, but he does not share Brunetto's political and ethical concerns.

The other author in whom Brunetto shows great interest is Boethius. The two rhetorical works from which Brunetto often quotes are

De differentiis topicis and *In topica Ciceronis.* The former was a very well-known text at the time Brunetto was writing his translation of Cicero. In it Boethius tries to find the differences between rhetoric and the other parts of philosophy, especially dialectics, and to establish a comparison between them by means of Aristotelian logical theory. The latter is a comparatively short commentary on Cicero's *Topica*, which explains the means by which one can find arguments in law courts.[32] Boethius's greatest work, *De consolatione philosophiae*, also offered Brunetto an attitude toward political justice that must have appealed to him as appropriate to his own situation.

Scholars have questioned Brunetto's direct knowledge of Sallust. He often quotes from *De coniuratione Catilinae*, and Catiline is certainly an important character in Brunetto's commentary, since he is represented as an epitome of what is ethically evil and politically dangerous: treachery, personal interest, corruption of his fellow countrymen, and pride. But Brunetto was certainly very well acquainted with another work, the French compilation *Li Fet des Romains*, where the story of Catiline's conspiracy is told at length. Brunetto uses this work in *Tresor* when he deals with Catiline, and it has often been assumed that this was his only source for the episodes that concern the conspiracy. In any case, to decide what source or sources Brunetto used is difficult since, like all medieval authors, he uses them with great freedom, often without citing them. We have very much the same situation with Lucan's *Bellum civile* or *Pharsalia*, many expressions of which appear to be directly translated into Italian in Brunetto's commentary but can also be found in *Li Fet des Romains* and with another important work, often attributed to William of Conches, *Moralium dogma philosophorum*, a series of maxims on Stoic ethics certainly known and widely employed by Brunetto.

Ovid, especially his *Heroides,* appears to be one of the important sources for Brunetto. He often quotes parts of the fictitious letters addressed by Dido, Medea, and other characters to their lovers. The direct speech makes the examples lively and immediate. Yet Brunetto's knowledge of the original has been questioned, for some of these quotations can be found in *Li Fet des Romains.* A possible re-elaboration of a line from the *Aeneid* (2.57–58) and a direct quotation from *Georgics* (4.1–5) call into question Brunetto's knowledge of Virgil. Although some scholars believe that Brunetto is unlikely to have had a direct knowledge especially of the *Georgics*, no intermediate source has been found, and the quotation is so precise that some sort of acquaintance with the Virgilian text ought perhaps to be assumed.

The question of sources is particularly complex in the case of medieval works, especially of medieval commentaries on the *De inventione* and *Rhetorica ad Herennium* and of treatises on epistolography. Commentaries on Cicero's works were frequently composed between the eleventh and the twelfh centuries. In France Brunetto found a well-established tradition, for William of Champeaux, Thierry of Chartres, and Peter Helias had promoted a revival of Roman rhetoric, while the work of Manegold of Lautenbach had slowly moved from the Rhineland to the north of France (Chartres, Laon, Reims) and had found its way down to Paris.[33]

Gian Carlo Alessio has shown, by means of a very detailed analysis, that an anonymous *Ars rhetorice* (Oxford, Bodleian Library, MS Canon. Class. Lat. 201), probably composed in Italy, is a direct source of *La rettorica* (and this may incidentally solve many problems about Brunetto's knowledge of classical and medieval sources).[34] Alessio compares the text in this manuscript to Brunetto's translation and commentary and argues that it is the most important source of *La Rettorica*, and that Brunetto may have had a copy of this text when composing his own. Similarly, Guido Baldassarri has compared a fragmentary comment by Theodoric of Chartres to the corresponding passage in *La rettorica*, which in turn depends on Grillio's commentary on *De inventione*.[35]

What seems certain is that in Paris Brunetto once more encountered the kind of culture and intellectual traditions he had probably experienced earlier at the University of Bologna, where rhetoric was not always Ciceronian in spirit and method, as the work of Boncompagno da Signa clearly shows.[36] Brunetto found these traditions perfectly consistent with his ideas about the city-state, the function of the *podestà*, and communal policy in general. This attitude must have come natural to one who had previously had great experience of civic life and was to have it again on returning to Florence. Until then somewhat neglected in academic *curricula*, Ciceronian rhetoric was witnessing a revival in the newly established city-states. One of Brunetto's contemporaries, the Florentine judge Bono Giamboni, translated and abridged the *Rhetorica ad Herennium*.[37] In this work, entitled *Fiore di rettorica*, perhaps after the work of Guidotto da Bologna, Bono shows an attitude not very different from Brunetto's, in that he translates and chooses what to translate and what to neglect very freely, retaining what he believes to be important and summarizing the rest. In his translation he does what Brunetto was doing in his commentary—that is, he uses his author to suit his own purposes, by giving his ideas the name of a well-known authority. Like Brunetto, Bono translates *res publica* as *comune* and *Senatus* as *consiglio*.[38] He thus makes it clear once more that republican Florence is the true heir of ancient Rome. Still, the forensic rhetoric of Bologna and the theoretical aspects discussed at Paris University did not exhaust the duties of the civic officer Brunetto had been before his exile and was to become again once back in Florence. The exchange of letters between the Florentine commune and its allies and enemies had become so important that the art of letter writing could not be neglected. Brunetto gave the *ars dictaminis* the same dignity he had given oratory and discussed it at length, starting from such sources as Guido Faba's *Summa dictaminis*, Boncompagno da Signa's *Quinque tabulae salutationum*, and, above all, Bene da Firenze's *Candelabrum*.[39] His translation of Cicero into the vernacular created the milieu from which French translations, such as Jean Antioche's translation of the *De inventione* and *Rhetorica ad Herennium* (1282), subsequently arose.[40]

Manuscripts

La rettorica survives in eight manuscripts.[41]

> Florence, Biblioteca Nazionale Centrale, Magliabechiano, II, II, 91 (m[1]): paper, folio, fifteenth century. *La rettorica* occupies fols. 1r–32v.

> Florence, Biblioteca Nazionale Centrale, Magliabechiano, II, IV, 73 (m): paper, folio, end of the fourteenth century. *La rettorica* occupies fols. 1r–43v.

> Florence, Biblioteca Nazionale Centrale, Magliabechiano, II, IV, 124 (M): paper, folio, mid-fifteenth century. M contains only *La rettorica* and is written by only one hand.

> Florence, Biblioteca Nazionale Centrale, Magliabechiano, II, IV, 127 (M[1]): parchment, quarto, fourteenth century. *La rettorica* occupies fols. 1r–41v. M[1] is written in two columns, and the translations from Cicero are in large letters, while Brunetto's commentary is in smaller ones (see *La rettorica* 2.6–9).

> Florence, Biblioteca Nazionale Centrale, Magliabechiano, II, VIII, 32 (m[2]): paper, quarto, fifteenth century. *La rettorica* occupies fols. 3v–58v.

> Florence, Biblioteca Nazionale Centrale, Laurenziano, XLIII, 19 (L): paper, folio, written in two columns, early fifteenth century. *La rettorica* occupies fols. 39r–82v.

> Florence, Biblioteca Medicea Laurenziana, Redi 23 (R): paper, folio. It belongs to the early fifteenth century and contains only

part of the text, folios 121v–133v, from the beginning to the end of Brunetto's commentary to paragraph 4. Discovered by Enrico Rostagno in 1915.

Munich, Bayerische Staatbibliothek, Cod. 1038 (formerly Cod. It. 148) (S): paper, folio, fifteenth century. The folios containing *La Rettorica* are 33r–42r.

Florence, Biblioteca Nazionale Centrale, Magliabechiano, II, II, 48: paper, folio, fifteenth century. Folios containing *La rettorica* are 1r–33v.

The *editio princeps* of *La rettorica* was printed in Rome in 1546 by the Florentine printer Francesco Serfranceschi. Two subsequent editions, little more than reprints of Serfranceschi's text, came out in Naples in 1851, edited by Michele Dello Russo, and in Florence in 1883. The latter has Brunetto's translation but not his commentary. In 1912 Ernesto Monaci included part of Brunetto's translation, edited by Pio Rajna, in his *Crestomazia italiana dei primi* secoli.[42] In 1915 Francesco Maggini prepared an accurate critical edition, with a collation of the six manuscripts he knew of (R and S were discovered later) but mainly based on M and M[1.] This has by now become the standard edition of *La rettorica*. In 1968 Cesare Segre revised Maggini's edition and reprinted it with a preface. This edition has been used for the present translation.[43]

Brunetto's style in *La rettorica* aims mainly at combining directness and clarity with a certain elegance, which allows him to compare indirectly his work with Cicero's. It is evident that he is trying to find—and often to create—the vernacular equivalent of Cicero's expressions. He does so not as a kind of archaeological research but as a way to show that the work of the great Roman rhetorician is well suited to the present situation of Florence as a city-state and to establish a tradition in the expressions concerning the subjects he is dealing with. Moreover, I think Brunetto's mainly paratactic syntax depends, first, on the fact that in the academic *curricula* rhetoric was part of logic and the aim of logic is demonstration; and, second, on his growing experience of French encyclopedias with their lists of items and their definitions. In spite of his practical purposes, however, Brunetto's language is the language of the academies and probably of most university lectures.

In this translation I have tried to give an account of Brunetto's style rather than imitate it, emphasizing the clarity of his exposition and his interest in unambiguous definitions. His prose was received as very modern and direct in his time and to give it what now to us seems an ancient flavor by rendering the paratactic syntax of the work literally would in all probability achieve the opposite effect of making the text heavy and difficult to follow. I have therefore chosen to adopt an academic prose and to give the utmost attention to the accurate rendering of Brunetto's technical terms and to the author's taxonomy in the subdivisions and diagram trees that abound in the text. Modern scholarship on Brunetto still focuses mainly on *Tresor*, but *La rettorica* is now recognized as an important work both from the point of view of the vernacular translation of Latin texts and of the revival of Cicero's *De inventione* at the birth of the city-republics.

NOTES

[1] Murphy, *Rhetoric in the Middle Ages*, p. 109.

[2] The *catena* gloss seems to have started in the eleventh century with the school of Lawrence of Amalfi; see Ward, "The Medieval and Early Renaissance Study of Cicero's *De inventione* and the *Rhetorica ad Herennium*," p. 20.

[3] The forms of public speech have been studied in detail by Artifoni, "I podestà professionali" and "Sull'eloquenza politica del Duecento italiano." The relationship between rhetoric and the government of the city-states is the subject of studies by Segre, *Lingua, stile e società*; Bartuschat, "La 'Rettorica' di Brunetto Latini"; and Tabasso, "Brunetto Latini." There is complete agreement among scholars that the connection is a very close one.

[4] Compagni, *Cronica* 2.20, ed. Luzzatto, p. 98. See Segre, *Lingua, stile e società*, p. 26; and Milner, "Communication, Consensus and Conflict."

[5] Mazzoni, "Latini, Brunetto."

[6] For the differences between Brunetto's ideas of language and history and those Dante develops in the *Commedia*, see Mazzotta, *Dante, Poet of the Desert*, pp. 66–106.

[7] Holloway, *Twice-Told Tales*, assumes that Brunetto is Dante's master and interprets sources like Villani literally.

[8] Alessio, "Brunetto Latini e Cicerone," believes that Brunetto is likely to have studied at Bologna both at the university and in some "notarial schools," where he could have acquired the necessary knowledge and skills that would later be useful to him in his profession. Inglese, in his biography of Brunetto Latini ("Latini Brunetto" [in *Letteratura italiana*]), also supports the idea that he may have studied at Bologna.

[9] Isidoro Del Lungo, a nineteenth-century historian and scholar with a deep knowledge of Florentine history, discovered various documents concerning Brunetto's life and published them as an appendix to Sundby, *Della vita e delle opera di Brunetto Latini*.

[10] Davidsohn, *Storia di Firenze*, trans. Klein, 2:134–38, considers Brunetto the best *dictator* of his time. In his opinion, the particularly well-written letter that provided an answer to the pope's interdict could have been written only by him. As a matter of fact, this is the only proof we have of the authorship of the letter. Brunetto Latini's hand is considered probable not only for stylistic reasons but also for the position Brunetto held within the Florentine commune.

[11] The authenticity of the letter by Brunetto's father has been questioned, but modern scholars consider it an authentic document. It was first published by Donati, "Lettere politiche del secolo XIII," p. 222.

[12] Davidsohn, *Storia di Firenze*, trans. Klein, 2.2:12. Carmody, editor of *Li Livres du Tresor de Brunetto Latini*, considers the return of Brunetto with Charles of Anjou not sufficiently proved (pp. 396–97). In any case, Brunetto was certainly in Florence in 1267.

[13] This opinion was expressed by Isidoro del Lungo in Sundby, *Della vita e delle opera di Brunetto Latini*, p. 207.

[14] Mazzoni, "Latini, Brunetto," p. 586, is anxious to show the affinities in destiny and political passion between Dante and Brunetto, although he does not believe that Brunetto was *strictu sensu* one of Dante's masters.

[15] Ceva, *Brunetto Latini*, p. 55, emphasizes the importance of Brunetto's intervention in the Consiglio dei Savi in favor of the authority of the Priori in a delicate military question.

[16] The date of Brunetto's death is generally believed to be 1294, as in Villani's account. A record in the Bologna State Archive moves Brunetto's death back to December 26, 1293; see Inglese, "Latini, Brunetto," p. 7, and Beltrami, p. ix.

[17] Rossi, "Observations sur l'origine et la signification du mot 'fablel.'" The connection with Boncompagno da Signa has been assumed by Sarina Nathan in her edition of *Amicitia*.

[18] Cesare Segre, in his analysis of "S'eo son distretto innamoratamente," argues that there is no proof of Brunetto's homosexuality, and that his being "against nature" must be interpreted allegorically; "S'eo son distretto innamoratamente," ed. Segre and Ossola, p. 138n. He recalls Dante's objection in *Convivio* 1.11 to those who despised the vernacular and wrote their works in other languages. Beltrami, p. xxxv, agrees with Segre. There is still considerable disagreement among scholars on this point. Those who believe that Dante should be interpreted literally remark, in accordance with Davis, "Brunetto Latini and Dante," that Dante met other sodomites in the canto. Others believe the vice incompatible with the respect and the affection the poet shows toward the Florentine rhetorician. A political reading of the canzone emphasizing the shared love for Florence is made by Armour, "The Love of Two Florentines." Robert Hollander offers an overview of readings of *Inferno* 15–16 and *Purgatorio* 26 in "Dante's Harmonious Homosexuals (*Inferno* 16.7–90)."

[19] Copeland and Sluiter, *Medieval Grammar and Rhetoric*, p. 755. When this book was published, my edition was almost finished, so that I could take a very limited account of this fine piece of work.

[20] Baldassarri, "Ancora sulle 'fonti' della 'Rettorica'"; Minnis, *Medieval Theory of Authorship*. On the *accessus*, see Quain, "The Mediaeval *Accessus ad auctores*." Brunetto adapts what Hunt, "The Introductions to the *Artes* in the Twelfth Century," calls a Type C *accessus*; see also Baldassarri, "'Prologo' e 'Accessus ad auctores'"; and Minnis, *Medieval Theory of Authorship*, pp. 17–28. In writing the second prologue in the form of an *accessus*, Brunetto provides himself with an audience of his own to read for the author's, intent, and other materials of a work.

[21] The idea that nobility lies in one's intellectual and moral qualities rather than in an illustrious descent is a commonplace, particularly in the poets of the Dolce stilnuovo. Dante emphasizes the concept in *Convivio*, 4.29; see Davis, "Brunetto Latini and Dante," p. 435.

[22] The relationship between rhetoric and ethics, which is so important in late medieval education, is consistent with the idea that nobility is not a matter of birth but of personal virtues; see Bartuschat, "La 'Rettorica' di Brunetto Latini," p. 39.

[23] Copeland, "The Ciceronian Rhetorical Tradition and Medieval Literary Theory," pp. 242–44.

[24] Mazzotta, *Dante, Poet of the Desert*, pp. 66–106, analyzes the concept of history in

Dante and shows that he ultimately rejects the idea of an absolute power of language by pointing out the ambiguities of rhetoric and of eloquence in general.

[25] Beltrami, p. xiv.

[26] Mazzotta, *Dante, Poet of the Desert*, pp. 78–79.

[27] This is an important point, for, if rhetoric is not only useful in law courts, it must nevertheless concern contention. Brunetto agrees with Cicero in rejecting Hermagoras's idea that rhetoric can be applied to all questions. Therefore, he can only extend the idea of contention to letters in order to argue that the laws of rhetoric are also valid for *dictamen*.

[28] Dionisotti, *Geografia e storia della letteratura italiana*, pp. 134–35, rejects the commonplace that Brunetto is a forerunner of humanism and the Renaissance. Sgrilli, "Retorica e società," equally questions this view and insists that the medieval tradition of Cicero's works did not imply a pre-humanistic attitude.

[29] Milner, "Communication, Consensus and Conflict," p. 396.

[30] Segre, *Lingua, stile e società*, pp. 218–19.

[31] Copeland and Sluiter, *Medieval Grammar and Rhetoric*, p. 105, remark that Victorinus transforms Cicero's civic and social interests into a Neoplatonic account of the soul.

[32] *Boethius' In Ciceronis Topica*, trans. Stump, pp. 8–9.

[33] Ward, "The Medieval and Early Renaissance Study of Cicero's *De inventione* and the *Rhetorica ad Herennium*," pp. 25–26, analyzes the development of rhetoric after the Fourth Lateran Council (1215).

[34] Alessio, "Brunetto Latini e Cicerone."

[35] Baldassarri, "'Prologo' e 'Accessus ad auctores.'"

[36] Boncompagno da Signa was a master at Bologna, and in all his works his aim is more practical than academic. He engaged in teaching his law students how to face trials and litigations. He often spoke against the method of the *Rhetorica ad Herennium* and was therefore considered anti-Ciceronian.

[37] Segre, *Lingua, stile e società*, pp. 299–300; Cox, "Ciceronian Rhetoric in Late Medieval Italy"; and Milner, "Communication, Consensus and Conflict," p. 374.

[38] Cox, "Ciceronian Rhetoric in Late Medieval Italy," p. 116.

[39] Guido Faba's *Summa dictaminis* is closely related to Bene da Firenze's *Candelabrum*, at least from the point of view of the doctrine, although his main source is *Rhetorica ad Herennium*, and he defines almost all the figures included in this treatise (Alessio, "Brunetto Latini e Cicerone,"). *Salutatio* was considered a distinctive feature of letters with respect to speeches delivered before an audience. Therefore, it was usually analyzed in great detail in dictaminal treatises. Bene da Firenze wrote his *Candelabrum* with the aim of explaining Cicero's rhetorical doctrine completely and faithfully. He reproduces part of the *Rhetorica ad Herennium* as well as the majority of the examples that can be found in that treatise. He may have had a commentary on *Ad Herennium* at his disposal, since some points can be found in Thierry de Chartres's commentary but not in the original (Alessio, 154).

[40] Copeland, "Translation."

[41] Beltrami, p. liv.

[42] Monaci, *Crestomazia italiana dei primi secoli*.

[43] Cesare Segre's revision is not very extensive, nor does it touch on essential points. Segre corrects some misprints and comments on some difficult points, but otherwise reproduces Maggini's edition without important modifications.

La rettorica

HERE BEGINS THE EXPOSITION of Rhetoric,[1] rendered into the vernacular from the books of Tullius and from those of many philosophers[2] by *Ser* Brunetto Latino,[3] Florentine. The larger letter refers to the text of Tullius, while the smaller one to the Commentator's.[4] The prologue[5] now begins.

1. Tullius

1. I have often deeply wondered whether eloquence and a passion for rhetoric have brought about greater good or evil to men and cities. In fact, when I consider the harm done to our Commune[6] and turn over in my mind the ancient adversities of the greatest cities, I see that no small part of these misfortunes has been caused by men who were endowed with great eloquence but little wisdom.

1. Here Speaks the Commentator[7]

1. Rhetoric is a twofold science. One of its branches is concerned with the art of speaking, and this is the subject of Tullius's book, while the other deals with the writing of letters, and this the Commentator will discuss as the book proceeds and place and time require, since Tullius does not discuss it explicitly in his treatise.[8]

2. Rhetoric, like the other sciences, can be taught in two ways: from the outside, so to speak, and from the inside.[9] From the outside, it is taught by showing what rhetoric is, what its genre, subject matter, task, parts, specific means, and aims are, and who practices it. This is what Boethius did in the fourth book of his *Topics*.[10] From the inside, the rules of the art are shown as far as speaking and letter writing are concerned, that is, we learn what the exordium, the narration, and the other parts should be like, whether in orations or epistles, i.e., dictated letters. Both are discussed by Tullius in this book. 3. However, since Tullius did not show either what

rhetoric is or who practices it, for the sake of clarity the Commentator is going to deal with both. 4. Rhetoric is a science of speaking well, that is to say, rhetoric is the science by means of which we can elegantly speak and write letters. It can also be defined as the science of speaking well about a chosen topic, through which we can ornately deal with a certain matter. An even more complete definition is possible: rhetoric is a science that allows us a full and perfect eloquence in public as well as in private controversies, that is, a science by which we shall be able to speak perfectly and exhaustively both on public and private questions: a competent and perfect speaker is certainly one who can use in his speech well-chosen words, full of good counsel. By public matters, we mean those where problems concerning cities or groups of people are at issue, while private ones concern the affairs of individuals. Throughout the Commentator intends to use for letter writing the same definitions he has used for oratory, since there may be those who are perfectly capable of writing letters but lack the courage or the ability to speak in public; on the other hand, whoever can speak well can also write letters appropriately. 5. Having defined rhetoric, we shall now turn to those who practice it. These are of two sorts: the *rector* and the *orator*.[11] Namely, the *rector* teaches the science according to the principles and the rules of the art. The orator, having learned the art well, makes good use of it in speaking and in writing letters on the appointed topics, as competent orators and letter writers do, among whom was Master Piero dalle Vigne, who, because of these qualities, became one of Emperor Frederick II's ministers and ruled over him and the Empire.[12] Therefore, Victorinus claims that an *orator*, that is, a speaker, is a man who is both good and experienced in the art of speaking and can employ full and perfect eloquence in public as well as in private controversies.[13]

6. After showing what rhetoric is and what kind of people practice it, one by teaching it, the other by actually delivering speeches, the Commentator will disclose who the author of the book is, i.e., who has composed it, and will show what his intention in writing it was; furthermore, he will discuss its subject matter, the reason why he wrote this book, how useful it can be, and what its title is.[14] 7. This work has two authors: one who composed his book on rhetoric both out of the precepts of all the philosophers who lived before him and from the vivid source of his own mind, that is, Marcus Tullius Cicero, the wisest among the Romans. The second is Brunetto Latino, Florentine, who put all his passion and learning into explaining and clarifying what Tullius had said. This is the person this book refers to as "the Commentator," that is, the one who expounds

and illustrates Tullius's book, both in his own words and in those of the ancient philosophers and masters, and as much more as is needed by the art of what was neglected in Tullius's book, as the careful reader will find in what follows.[15] 8. In this book Brunetto proposes to instruct the person for the love of whom he engaged in the writing of this treatise on the art of speaking elegantly on any suggested topic.[16] 9. The Commentator will follow the organization of Tullius's book in dealing with the five general parts of rhetoric, namely, *inventio*, i.e., finding how to develop the proposed subject, and the other four parts which can be found in the second book which Tullius dedicated to his friend Herennius, of which what is convenient will be mentioned.[17] 10. This book owes its existence to the fact that Brunetto Latino, because of the war between the two Florentine factions, was exiled from his city when the Guelph faction, which had sided with the pope and with the Church of Rome, was expelled and banished from the land.[18] He then went to France to attend to his business, and there he found a friend from the same city and of the same political party, a very rich man, extremely well-mannered and of great wisdom, who received him with great honor and proved to be so helpful that Brunetto would call him "his harbor," as can clearly be seen in many parts of this book.[19] This man was a naturally excellent speaker and anxious to learn about the wisest people's ideas about rhetoric: it was for his sake that Brunetto Latino, who was well versed in letters and greatly devoted to the study of rhetoric, began to write this book, where he first gives a translation of Tullius's book because of its great authority, then adding, wherever necessary, material from his own knowledge and from that of other scholars. 11. This book is extremely useful in that whoever masters its precepts and the rules of the art will be able to speak exhaustively on a suggested matter. 12. The title of this book, as can be seen from the introduction, is *Here Begins the Exposition of Rhetoric Rendered into the Vernacular from the Books of Tullius and from Those of Many Philosophers*. That the title is suitable and very appropriate is clearly shown by the work itself, since Tullius's book has actually been translated into the vernacular and highlighted by the larger letter, as a mark of its greater importance and dignity, while the smaller letter refers to the opinions of many philosophers and to those of the Commentator. Here the writer leaves this subject to go back to the actual exposition of the text. 13. In this section the Commentator explains how Tullius, wishing to rescue rhetoric from the low esteem in which it was held at the time he was writing and make it loved and cherished, wrote a prologue, as wise people do, purging those things that he judged to be detrimental. This is exactly what Boethius recommends in his commentary on *Topics*, i.e., that whoever writes on any subject should first discard what he believes to be too grievous.[20] So Tullius did when he purged three grievous matters: firstly, the harmful consequences of eloquence; secondly, Plato's opinion; and thirdly, Aristotle's judgement. Plato claimed that rhetoric is not art, but nature, since he knew of many who were naturally good speakers but had had no instruction in the art. Aristotle, instead, believed rhetoric to be art, but an evil one, since eloquence seemed to him to have caused more harm than good to communes and to individuals.[21] 14. Therefore, purging these three grievous issues, Tullius proceeds as follows: he first says that he has thought deeply and for a long time about the effects produced by eloquence; in the second part of the prologue, he shows the good and the evil that derived from it and which of them prevailed; in the third part, he discusses three topics. Firstly, he says what he thinks of wisdom; secondly, he gives his opinion about eloquence; and thirdly, he deals with wisdom and eloquence taken together. In the fourth part, he offers a demonstration of what he has said about the first three points and concludes by closely arguing in favor of the study of rhetoric from the point of view of what is honorable, useful, possible, and necessary. In the fifth part, Tullius shows what he is going to deal with in this book and how he intends to proceed. 15. Having said at the beginning how often and how long he has thought about the good and the evil of rhetoric, Tullius first brings up evil, since he is perfectly aware that one recent evil is much more present to people's minds than all the past good.[22] Therefore, professing not to remember the former good, he pretends to blame the science of rhetoric in order to be able to praise and defend it with greater determination. 16. Thus we can clearly understand that the very words he uses to describe those damages caused by eloquence that cannot be concealed are in fact a defense of it, since they temper and minimize its evil consequences. In fact, where he speaks of "damages," he does it in such a way that they appear to be slight hurts to which people hardly give a second thought; when he says "of our Commune," he automatically belittles the evil, since people are much more interested in their own harm than in their Commune's; when I say "our Commune,"[23] I mean Rome, since Tullius was a Roman citizen, a plebeian of no great standing,[24] but, because of his wisdom, he was held in such high repute that everybody stood by his word. He lived at the time of Catiline, Pompey, and Julius Caesar when, for the good of the country, he was fiercely opposed to Catiline. In the war between Caesar and Pompey he sided with Pompey, as did all the wise people who loved the city of

Rome. He calls it "our Commune" perhaps because Rome, which rules all over the world, is every man's Commune. 17. When he says "the past adversities," he also lessens the evil, since we tend to disregard old harms. The same he does when he says "the greatest cities" since, in the words of our fine poet Lucan, the greatest things are not allowed to last long;[25] and the other poet[26] says that the greatest things fall under their own weight.[27] Thus, eloquence does not appear to be the cause of the evil that befalls the greatest cities. When he says that harm has been caused by people who had great eloquence but no wisdom, he evidently minimizes the evil and defends rhetoric, since the harm is ascribed to eloquent but unwise people, not to eloquence itself. "This word 'eloquence,'" Victorinus maintains, "has a good ring to it, nor can evil come out of good."[28] 18. This is really a fine color of rhetoric, to defend while pretending to blame, and to accuse while pretending to praise. This figure of speech is called *insinuatio* and will be dealt with in this book in due course. Here the report moves away from the first part of the prologue, where Tullius has expressed his thoughts and discussed the evils brought about by eloquence. He now turns in the second part to the good that eloquence has produced.

2. Tullius

1. When I undertake to retrieve from the ancient records things that are now far from our remembrance because of their antiquity, I find that eloquence, with the help of reason, that is, with wisdom, has made it easier to conquer and build cities, to quench many battles, to establish sound alliances, and to form most holy friendships.

2. The Commentator

1. After mentioning the evils produced by eloquence, now Tullius proceeds to single out its good aspects, and he finds that these are much more numerous than the others, because he is more intent on praising rhetoric than on blaming it. It should be noticed that he says "eloquence combined with wisdom," in that the will to do good comes from wisdom and the ability to act accordingly derives from eloquence. 2. The other words in the text, namely, "to build cities and to quench many battles," are mentioned in the appropriate order, since men first gathered to live under the same laws with honest habits and to increase their possessions; then, after they had become rich, envy began to rise among them, and with envy came wars and battles. The wise orators, then, extinguished battles, and

men later formed associations to do business together and to practice commerce; and from these associations strong friendships arose by means of eloquence and wisdom.[29] 3. However, just to explain the meaning of these words, for the sake of clarity, it is appropriate to show what a city is, who can be called a companion or a friend, what wisdom and eloquence are, since the Commentator does not wish to leave a single word the meaning of which is not fully explicated:

4. *What a city is.*[30] A city is a gathering of people who have come together to live according to reason; thus, people cannot be called citizens of the same Commune merely because they live together within the same city walls, but only if they agree to live according to the same rules.

5. *What a companion is.* A companion is one connected to another person by some sort of covenant aimed at achieving a certain result; of these people Victorinus says that if they are steadfast, eloquence makes them even steadier.

6. *What a friend is.* A friend is whoever, because of a similar way of life, establishes with another person a relationship based on a bond of honest and faithful love. Namely, to be called friends two people must have the same habits and lead similar lives: he says "similar lives" and "honest love" to maintain that friendship should have nothing to do with lust or equally filthy things, and he says "faithful love" in order to exclude from it all personal interest or advantage, and attribute it only to steadfast virtue. It is therefore evident that friendship based on personal interest or dishonest pleasure cannot be a truthful one but is debased by these vices.

7. *What wisdom is.* Wisdom is the understanding of the real truth of things.

8. *What eloquence is.* Eloquence is the ability to utter polished speeches full of fine counsel.

3. Tullius

1. Reason itself led me—who had long been meditating[31]—to this unquestionable conclusion, that wisdom without eloquence is of little use to cities, while eloquence without wisdom is often very dangerous and never helpful. Therefore, whoever neglects the most righteous and honest study of philosophy and ethics, devoting all his efforts to the practice of eloquence alone, is certainly a citizen useless to himself and dangerous to his city and country. On the contrary, a man who arms himself with eloquence, not to take up arms against the good of his country but to fight for it, seems to me a very helpful man and citizen, truest to his own interests and to those of his country.[32]

3. The Commentator

1. After completing the first two parts of the prologue, Tullius begins the third, where three main topics are discussed. He first says what he thinks about wisdom, up to the word "therefore"; in the second part, he gives his opinion about eloquence; in the third part, beginning with the words "a man who arms himself," both wisdom and eloquence are discussed in their mutual relationship. 2. On this Victorinus says: "If we wish something to be done quickly in our cities, we need wisdom and eloquence operating together, since wisdom alone is always slow of action."[33] This is evident whenever someone is wise but not a good speaker: if we asked him for advice, he would not be as quick in giving it as he would if he were an eloquent speaker. If, on the contrary, he were both wise and eloquent, he would be able to make anything he liked appear reliable. 3. When Tullius mentions those who neglect the study of philosophy and ethics, I take "philosophy" to mean "wisdom" and "ethics" to indicate those virtues such as courage, righteousness, and the other ones, the assignment of which is to make us prudent, just, and honest. 4. On the other hand, whoever, disregarding wisdom and virtue, pursues only the achievement of eloquence will end up by not really believing what he says, thereby causing harm and injury to himself and to his country, since he will be unable to look after either private or public welfare in the appropriate time, place, or sequence of actions. 5. Therefore, whoever arms himself with eloquence is useful to himself and to his country. By "arms," I allude to eloquence, by "wisdom," I mean force; in fact, just as by the arms we defend ourselves from our enemies and by force we oppose their arms,[34] in the same way by eloquence we defend our case against our opponent, and by wisdom we restrain from statements potentially harmful to us. So much for the third part of Tullius's prologue. 6. We now proceed to the fourth section of the prologue in order to prove what has been said before and to arrive at the conclusion that rhetoric should be studied to achieve both eloquence and wisdom. This is very closely argued by Tullius, so that we are persuaded that it can and should be as he says, that it is appropriate that is should be so, that it is right that it should be so. Here is Tullius's text, in larger letters, followed by the comment in smaller ones, after the book's fashion.

4. Tullius

1. Thus, if we wish to account for the origin of eloquence, whether it was achieved by art, study, custom, or force of nature, we shall find that it

originated in the worthiest of motives and flourished because of excellent reasons. For there was a time when men wandered about the fields like animals and went through their lives like wild beasts, everybody acting under the impulse of the body rather than according to the guidance of the mind; moreover, at that time neither holy religion nor human duties were honored. No legitimate marriage existed, nor could anybody boast of sure offspring: the advantages of reason and equity were completely unknown. Therefore, by error and ignorance, covetousness, that blind and foolhardy master of the soul, in order to be able to act after its own will, misused physical strength with the help of the worst possible companions.

4. The Commentator

1. In the fourth part of the prologue, Tullius, wishing to demonstrate that eloquence arises and flourishes for excellent causes and very honorable reasons, explains that there was a time when men were coarse and ignorant like beasts: man—philosophers maintain and the Holy Scripture confirms—is composed of body and of rational soul, this one having a complete knowledge of things because of the reason it is endowed with. 2. Therefore, Victorinus says: "Just as the power of wine is weakened by the vessel that holds it, in the same way the soul's strength changes according to the properties of the body it is united with";[35] so, if the body has an evil disposition and is oppressed with negative humors, the soul, because of the body's burden, loses the apprehension of things and becomes hardly capable of distinguishing between good and evil, as it occurred in past times to the souls of many who, under the burden of the bodies, were so false and ill-advised that they knew neither God nor themselves. Thus, they misused their bodily strength by murdering one another, stealing or taking other people's property by brute force, living in lust, unable to recognize their own children or having legitimate wives. 3. But nature, that is, God's will, had not distributed that wild disposition equally among men: there was a wise and extremely eloquent man who, seeing that men could use reason, began to talk to them in order to acquaint them with the knowledge of God, with the love of Him, and of their own fellow-men, as the Commentator will explain in due course. This is why Tullius says that eloquence originated in honorable motives and excellent reasons, that is, for the love of God and of one's fellow men, without which mankind would not have survived. 4. Where the text says that men wandered in the fields, I take it to mean that they had neither house nor places to stay at, but went about like animals. 5. Where it says that they lived like beasts, I believe this means

that they used to eat raw meat, uncooked herbs, and other food of the kind beasts feed on. 6. Where he says "they did almost everything by brute force rather than by reason," I notice he says "almost" to mean that not everything was done out of force, but in some actions men followed reason and common sense, for example, when they spoke, yearned for something, or did other things that come from the soul. 7. When he says that the holy religion of God was not worshipped, I take it that they were not aware of the existence of God. 8. Where he mentions human duties, I intend that these men were unable to live according to moral principles and did not know prudence, justice, or other virtues. 9. Where he says that they were unable to follow reason, I interpret "reason" as "justice," which, according to the law books, can be defined as the constant and firm will to give everybody what is due to him. 10. Where he says "equity," I take it to mean that the same punishment is given for the same crime both to eminent and to humble people. 11. Where he says "covetousness," I intend the vice opposite to temperance, which induces people to yearn for things one should not long for, thrusts an evil power into our soul, and prevents it from rejecting evil inclinations. 12. Where he mentions "ignorance," I think he means that they were unable to tell the difference between what is useful and what is useless: this is why he says that covetousness is blind because of ignorance, and because it does not distinguish advantages from damages. 13. Where he says "foolhardy," he alludes to men who are bold and rash enough to do what should not be done. 14. Where he says "misused their physical strength," I mean that they were not using it properly, for, as Victorinus says, our physical strength was given us by God to be employed in useful and honorable proceedings, but they did exactly the opposite.[36] 15. After the Commentator has illustrated the origin of eloquence in Tullius's text, he will show how rhetoric first came to be and developed.

5. Tullius

1. There was at that time a great and wise man who was soon aware of the potential disposition toward great enterprises existing in men if only one could induce them to establish and obey rules capable of improving their behavior. So he gathered and got together all those who were scattered here and there about the fields and in wild hiding places and taught them what is useful and honest, and although they at first, being unused to such things, considered them too hard to follow, later they began to listen to him carefully as he spoke well and wisely, so that he was able to transform their original fierceness and cruelty into humbleness and meekness.

5. The Commentator

1. In this section Tullius intends to show who began eloquence, how it started, and what it concerned. And this is his theme: at the time when people lived in such bad circumstances, there was a man of great eloquence and wisdom who realized that the human disposition, that is, the reason mankind naturally possesses and that allows men to understand and reflect, together with the inclination to perform the greatest feats, such as keeping peace, loving God and the other creatures, building cities, castles, mansions, adopting honest habits, promoting justice among their fellow-men, and living lawfully, could be directed if someone could be found who was able to guide them, taking them away from their wild lives, and improving their behavior by means of rules, that is, precepts, laws, and statutes capable of keeping them under control.[37] 2. Here a problem arises, for someone could ask: "How could they be made better, if they were not even good?" The answer is that their soul was naturally good and could be improved, as indicated above. 3. Thus, this wise man forced—and Tullius says "forced" because they did not at first want to come together—them to assemble, and he says "brought them together," since they later agreed to come together. For this wise man strove so much by wisdom and eloquence, showing them the best of reasons and the prospective advantages, using his own wealth to provide them with good food, fine dinners, excellent suppers, and so many other pleasures, that they were persuaded to come together and listen to his words. And he used to teach them all that is useful, such as: "Stick together, help one another and you will be protected and strong; also, build cities and villages." Moreover, he used to tell them what is honorable: "Let the meaner honor his better, and the son fear his own father, etc.," he kept saying. 4. Although at first living according to reason and law seemed very hard to those who had been used to a wild life and had been born in absolute freedom, so that they loathed to be subjected to others, little by little, by listening to the fine eloquence of that wise man and considering in their minds that a great and total freedom to do evil would soon turn against themselves and end up in their destruction as well as endanger the whole mankind, began to listen to him and to endeavor to understand what he was telling them. In this manner, that wise man was able to rescue them from their fierceness and cruelty. Tullius says "fierceness" since they used to live like wild animals, and he says "cruelty" because father and son did not know each other, but, rather, they were likely to kill each other; he made them humble and meek, that is, capable of following reason and virtue and of being opposed to evil.

5. After saying who began eloquence, to whom it was addressed, and how it was first practiced, Tullius is going to explain the means without which its aims could not have been achieved.

6. Tullius

1. Therefore, it seems to me that wisdom alone, silent and scanty of words, could hardly have managed to achieve so much, that is, to turn so quickly people away from their ancient and long-drawn habits, to cast them into completely different stations in life.

6. The Commentator

1. In this section Tullius illustrates the means without which that wise man could not have attained what he did, and he calls "silent wisdom" the one of those who teach by deeds rather than by words, as hermits do. He also calls "scanty of words" the wisdom of those people who are unable to embellish it with fine words full of conceits in order to make others share their opinions. From this we can see that the power of wisdom without eloquence is scarce, and we can learn that wisdom combined with eloquence is the most powerful thing on earth. 2. Where he says "so quickly," I understand that that wise man could have achieved the same results by wisdom alone but not as quickly and in such a short time as he did by means of both wisdom and eloquence. Where he says "in different stations in life," I intend that one was made a knight, another a clerk, and others were directed to different occupations.

7–8. Tullius

1. After cities and villages had been built, men began to learn faithfulness, to submit to justice, to obey one another of their own will, and not only were they prepared to suffer pain and distress for the common good but also to lose their lives to defend it; this could not have been done if wise men had been unable to show people and make them believe by means of words, that is, by eloquence, what they had found out and come to believe themselves because of their wisdom. 8. Certainly, whoever was strong and powerful enough to rule over others would scarcely have accepted becoming equal to those he could dominate had not a wise and meek eloquence persuaded him to do so; so pleasant the former habits had been and of such old standing that they seemed to have become, in those men, almost

a second nature. Thus, I believe this was the ancient origin of eloquence, which then rose to the greatest heights and became extremely helpful to men in matters both of peace and of war.

7–8. The Commentator

1. In this section Tullius remarks that what wisdom alone would not have been able to achieve was obtained when it acted in association with eloquence. The matter is therefore as follows: as has been said before, men were brought together, taught how to do good, and to love one another, so they built cities and villages; and after cities had been established, men began to learn faithfulness. 2. By this, I mean that people can be called faithful who do not deceive their fellow men, nor do they admit of strife or conflict in the cities but endeavor to stop them if they happen to arise. Faith—a wise man said—is hope in what has been promised;[38] in legal terms, faith is what one promises and the other keeps. In another of his books, *On Duties*, Tullius defines faith as the foundation of justice, and says that it consists of truthfulness in speaking and steadfastness in promises.[39] This is the virtue called trustworthiness. 3. To such a great extent does Tullius praise eloquence joined to wisdom that he believes that otherwise the greatest achievements would not have been possible, and he adds that in that way it has done a great deal of good both in wartime and in peace.[40] This I take to mean that all affairs, of the Communes and of individuals alike, are of two kinds and pertain either to peace or to war, and in both situations rhetoric is so necessary that without it neither of them could be preserved.

9. Tullius

1. However, when men learned eloquence, following some sort of false virtue without any perception of moral duties, they put all their intelligence to evil intents, so that cities degenerated and the lives of people were included in such deterioration. Thus, after disclosing how the good began, we now proceed to explain how this evil started.

9. The Commentator

1. After Tullius has discussed all the good that has come from eloquence, he is now going to deal with all the harm that eloquence without wisdom has caused, but since he mainly intends to praise it, he ascribes the harm

to those who use it badly, rather than to eloquence itself. 2. He argues as follows: there have been foolish men with no discretion who, seeing that some people had achieved great honors and a high position in life because of their competent and appropriate use of eloquence, endeavored to become eloquent while totally neglecting the acquisition of wisdom, to the point that, just because their great eloquence was not accompanied by wisdom, they started riots and brought destruction to cities and Communes, and began to corrupt men's lives; this occurred because they looked as if they possessed wisdom, which they were totally divested and devoid of. 3. Victorinus says that eloquence alone is called "appearance," because it looks like wisdom, which induces people to believe that it dwells in those men where it actually does not abide.[41] These are those people who speak without any feeling for what is good, in order to obtain honors and advantages from the Communes. In such ways, they cause cities to become unsettled and drive people toward evil customs. 4. Then Tullius says: "After showing how the good that has derived from eloquence began, it is now convenient that the origin of the evil that came from it should be accounted for." And he goes on as follows:

10–13. Tullius on the Origin of the Evil Derived by Eloquence

1. It certainly seems likely to me that there was a time when people who possessed no eloquence and those who were less than wise did not usually meddle with public matters, while the wise and the eloquent did not interfere with private issues. So, in spite of the fact that there were excellent men who decided about the most important matters, I believe that there were others, cunning and shrewd, who used to deal with the petty controversies of private people; and since in these squabbles men were often firm in their lies and strongly opposed to truth, their incessant speaking made them bold. 2. Therefore, to defend their citizens from injuries, rulers were compelled to oppose themselves to these bold people, and everyone was forced to look after his own interests; as a consequence of this, those who were possessed only of eloquence without wisdom often seemed equally worthy or, at times, better than those who had both eloquence and wisdom; they were therefore considered by the crowd and considered themselves to be worthy of ruling over states. 3. And certainly it was not without justice that, once foolhardy and shameless people had become rulers, the greatest and most terrible storms should often take place; therefore, eloquence

came to be the object of such hatred and envy that the most excellent minds, as if running away from a gloomy storm to seek a safer harbor, withdrew to quieter studies, thus turning away from a life of turmoil and discord. As a consequence of their withdrawal, other honest and righteous studies appear to have been constantly pursued, thereby attaining great consideration. 4. The study of rhetoric was therefore abandoned almost by everybody and came to nothing at the very time it should have forcefully been kept alive and earnestly allowed to develop; for the more an honorable and righteous practice was misused and spoiled by the impudence and the boldness of foolhardy people, with such great harm to the Commune, the more appropriate it would have been to oppose all this and offer governments and cities advice and support. From this neither our Cato, Laelius, nor their disciple African, nor his grandsons, the Gracchi, retreated, since in these men there was supreme virtue, and their authority was increased by their supreme virtue; therefore, their eloquence was a great asset to themselves and great help and protection for the Commune.

10–13. The Commentator

1. In this section Tullius shows how the two evils he mentions, namely, the harm caused to the welfare of the cities and the corruption of the good lives and customs of the people, could take place; and although his text is written in such plain words that everybody can easily understand it, for the sake of greater clarity, the Commentator will add some words. 2. It is as follows: eloquence had placed wise and sensible rhetoricians so high that cities and Communes were ruled and public matters were dealt with by their advice; they sat in important offices, received great honors and performed great deeds without meddling either with private controversies, that is, with the affairs of individual men or with minor jobs or petty business. There were, however, two other kinds of men: those who were not good speakers, and those who had no wisdom but could well cry aloud and tell a lot of tales. These ones did not engage in public matters, that is, in those concerning states, official duties, and things important to Communes, but meddled with the petty affairs of private people, that is, of individuals. 3. Among them there were some, cunning and shrewd, whose deceitfulness and slyness were often mistaken for wisdom; they got into the habit of talking so much that by crying out and uttering so many words about the affairs of private people, they grew more and more pretentious and dared speak in a sort of mock eloquence, so much and so dishonestly that they firmly supported lies and false reasoning against

truth. 4. Therefore, to counterbalance the great evils that derived from such situations, the great people, i.e., the wise orators who were responsible for the important enterprises, were compelled to demean themselves by dealing with the petty affairs of private people in order to defend their friends and oppose the boldness of the others. Bold people are, however, of two sorts: some undertake great enterprises guided by reason, and these are the wise ones; while others venture into big projects without the guidance of reason, and this is the foolish kind of boldness. 5. Therefore, in their opposition, the good and wise people used to speak with justice, while the foolhardy ones, unacquainted with wisdom but possessed only with some eloquence, used to scream and bellow, unashamed of lying or of uttering evidently wrong statements, so that sometimes they were believed to be of equal, if not greater, wisdom and eloquence. The result was that the judgment of the mob, which, not coming from reason, is of no value, or perhaps the opinion these people had of themselves, which amounts to nothing, declared them worthy of presiding over important public affairs, so that they were made to rule over cities, perform the duties, and enjoy the honors connected to the government of the Communes. 6. No wonder, then, if states were struck by huge and very terrible storms. And note that he says "Huge" to refer to the quantity and to the fact that they last for a very long time, and he says "very terrible" to indicate the quality, since they were dire and dangerous, even causing the death of people;[42] and he says "storm," which is a simile, because just as a ship happens to find itself in a seastorm, and at times the waves are so high that it perishes, so can a city find itself in the same predicament because of conflicts, and at times they swell to such a degree that they cause it to perish and be destroyed. 7. For this reason eloquence came to be much hated and envied, hatred being nothing else than long-harbored anger, as is to be expected of good and wise people who had long been angry seeing those foolhardy men rule over cities; envy is nothing else than grief felt for other people's good fortune.[43] Therefore, the good and wise were extremely sorry to see those men engage in big undertakings and be greatly honored. 8. So those who had goodness as well as great intelligence withdrew from such enterprises and devoted themselves to quieter studies in order to avoid the turmoil of that kind of life and take shelter in a safer harbor. But mind that when Tullius says "of great intelligence," he implies that they might well have been able to oppose those foolhardy people, and were justly to be blamed because they did not. When he says "quieter studies," he intends the other philosophical disciplines such as those investigating the nature of divine as well as of human matters, e.g., ethics, which deals with virtues and customs; he calls those studies "quieter," since they have nothing to do with speaking in public, and this allowed the wise people to keep away from the uproar of the rabble. He further speaks of "the turmoil of that life," as it often occurred that in cities men were attacked with weapons and sometimes killed. 9. Therefore, eloquence, neglected by wise men, was once more reduced to nothing, being neither cared for nor appreciated. On the contrary, the other branches of philosophy cultivated by these people flourished and were held in great honor. 10. Tullius therefore blames those wise men who neglected eloquence at the very time it would have needed greater consideration because of the evil caused to the states by those foolish and boisterous men, who harmed the most honest and straightforward of sciences, i.e., eloquence, which is concerned with the most honorable and truthful matters. 11. Our Cato certainly did not turn away from it, nor did the other wise men who honestly cared for the Commune and were both wise and eloquent; on the contrary, they steadily advised and defended the state from those foolhardy babblers. So they were honored and held in such great consideration that whatever they said had the value of a sentence. This is why Tullius says that they had authority, a condition where one is both honored and feared. This is where the story stops and the author concludes once more that for good and honorable as well as feasible and necessary motives, eloquence should be studied, and he praises it in many ways.[44]

14. Tullius Concludes That Rhetoric Should Be Studied

14. For this reason, to my mind the fact that many people misuse eloquence in public as well as in private matters does not imply that it should be pursued with less diligence; on the contrary, it should be studied more accurately in order to prevent villains from attaining too much power to the harm of honest people and to everybody's ruin. Above all, it is also absolutely true that rhetoric concerns all things, both public and private, and that through it life is made safe, honorable, celebrated, and pleasant; from it many useful things befall to the Communes provided the moderating effects of wisdom are also present. From it, praise, honor, and dignity come to those who have achieved it; from it, friends obtain most certain and constant help.

14. The Commentator

1. The subject of this passage in Tullius's book is as follows: given that there are evil people who misuse eloquence, from that, in my opinion, it does

not follow that eloquence should be neglected, since evil men should not be allowed to acquire the power to harm the honest people and to bring destruction upon everybody. And note that those men who used to be in high positions and had great wealth were literally destroyed, and were ruined to the point of being reduced to the condition of beggars.[45] 2. Tullius then praises rhetoric, which concerns both Communes and individuals and makes men safe in that they can deal with controversies in such a way that you could scarcely find one capable of opposing them; then their life becomes honorable, that is, they are appreciated by those who know them; celebrated, that is, greatly valued by strangers; pleasant, since they lead a pleasing life, wise speakers being agreeable to themselves and to others. 3. Moreover, eloquence is greatly helpful to Communes, on condition that wisdom be nearby, that is, if it is joined to eloquence. Tullius also says that wisdom has a moderating effect on all matters since it can foresee the consequences of actions, devise for everything a certain method and a well-defined aim. He further states that people who possess eloquence and wisdom are praised, feared, and loved, and that their friends can find in them great and certain help, so that there is scarcely anybody who can oppose them, since they can speak consistently and wisely. He says "certain and constant" because a good and wise man cannot be corrupted for love, money, or for anything else. Here he ends with one last conclusion:

15. Tullius's Conclusion

1. It seems to me that men, who are in so many respects inferior to animals and weaker than them, in this one aspect are superior, and that is in the possession of speech. Therefore, whoever surpasses the other men in that very quality in which men surpass animals seems to me to achieve a noble and excellent condition.

15. The Commentator

1. In this section the issue is as follows: it is true that men are inferior to animals and weaker than them in many respects; for example, the elephant and many other animals have certainly bigger bodies than man; the lion and many other animals are surely stronger; moreover, the five senses of some animals are sharper than those of man. The boar's hearing, the lynx's sight, the monkey's sense of taste, the vulture's sense of smell, the spider's touch are certainly sharper than man's. But man surpasses all beasts and animals in one feature, that is, the power of speech. Therefore,

the man who can speak better than the others attains the very best of all good qualities.[46]

16. Tullius Announces What He Is Going to Deal With

1. This superior ability, that is, eloquence, cannot be obtained merely by nature or habit but must be acquired through instruction, as well. Therefore, it seems to be not inappropriate to analyze the rules set by those who devised them. However, before we illustrate the rules of rhetoric, the nature of the art should be explained together with its aims, functions, subject matter, and parts. For once these are known and acquired, more easily and quickly will everybody's mind be able to understand the scope and method of that art.

16. The Commentator

1. After praising rhetoric and dwelling on its praise in many ways, Tullius goes back to explain what he will deal with in his book. But first he gives some brilliant demonstrations so that everybody's mind can be better disposed to understand what will come. So he brings the prologue to an end and comes to the heart of the matter as follows:

17. After Concluding the Prologue, Tullius Begins to Deal with Eloquence

1. There is an organization of cities that has many great and important requirements, among which a very significant and considerable part is played by that kind of formalized eloquence that is called rhetoric. As a matter of fact, we agree neither with those who do not believe eloquence to be necessary to the policy of cities nor with those who believe that such policy wholly depends on the power and the art of the orators. Therefore, we shall define the art of rhetoric as part of the science of politics, that is, of the science of ruling over cities.

17. The Commentator

1. In this section of his book Tullius proceeds to demonstrate in the right order what he had promised to do at the end of the prologue. First of all, he defines the genus of the art, but, before going on, the Commentator will explain what is meant by "genus," so that the rest may be more easily grasped. 2. Almost everything can be said to be either general, in that it

includes many other things, or part of something general. For instance, the word "man" is general since it includes many people, i.e., Peter, John, etc., while the word "Peter" is a part. Similarly, in a more current way, "genus" can be understood as "ancestry," for if one mentions "the Tosinghi," this refers to the whole family tree, but if one says "Davizzo," this refers only to a part, that is, a man belonging to that family.[47] 3. Therefore, Tullius defines the genus of rhetoric in order to show its foundations as well as its nature. He maintains that the organization and the life of cities, of Communes as well as of individuals, have many important requirements concerning both deeds and words. 4. In the organization of cities, deeds involve what can be made by means of hands and feet, such as the arts of smiths, tailors, weavers; words concern rhetoric and the other disciplines related to speech. Therefore, the science of politics is general and includes rhetoric, i.e., the art of speaking well, as one of its parts.[48] 5. Before going on, however, the Commentator, believing that the science of politics is itself part of an even more general science, i.e., philosophy, will briefly define philosophy in order to show how noble and eminent the science of politics is, after which the excellence of rhetoric is also automatically proved. 6. Philosophy is that sovereign science which includes all the other disciplines. Its name is composed of two Greek words, the first is *phylos*, which is equivalent to "love"; the second is *sophya*, which means "wisdom," so that the meaning of philosophy is "love of wisdom." Therefore, nobody can be a philosopher if he does not love wisdom to the point of neglecting everything else in order to devote himself completely to the acquisition of it. A wise man defines philosophy as the inquiry into natural things, the knowledge of divine and human matters, as far as their interpretation is accessible to human beings.[49] Another wise man defines philosophy as an honest life, a passion for virtue, a *memento* of death, and a contempt for the world.[50] 7. Notice that defining something is saying what it is in words that do not apply to anything else; and, as such, if you use them in a different order, they still mean the same thing. In order to make this clear, let us look, by way of example, at the definition of "man," which is "a rational animal doomed to death."[51] No doubt these words pertain to man, nor could they be said of anything else, whether beast, bird, or fish, since these creatures are not endowed with reason. Now, if you put it in a different way and ask "Who is the rational animal doomed to death?" you can answer nothing else but "man." 8. It is true that in older times, because of their ignorance, men worried about three problems they were doubtful about, and not without reason, since all sciences revolve around these issues: the first problem concerned what man should do and what he should avoid; the second was why he should do some things and avoid others; the third was how to get to know the natures of all existing things. Since there were three issues, the wise philosophers decided to divide philosophy into three branches, namely metaphysics, practice, and logic, as the following diagram shows:

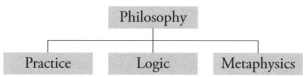

9. The first of these branches, i.e., practice, answers the first question on what man should do and what he should avoid. 10. The second, i.e., logic, provides an answer to the second problem and shows why some things must be done and others avoided; it is in turn divided into three parts, namely, dialectics, ephidics, and sophistry. The first concerns the art of questioning and arguing, and this is dialectics.[52] The second shows how to demonstrate one of the theses by means of truthful arguments, and this is called ephidics;[53] the third explains how to demonstrate what somebody has stated by means of dishonest arguments and false reasoning, and this is sophistry. The partition is shown in the following diagram:

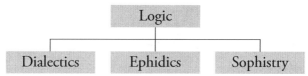

11. The third science, i.e., metaphysics, shows the natures of all existing things, and since there are three of them, it is convenient that this science should be divided into three branches, namely, theology, physics, and mathematics, according to the following diagram:

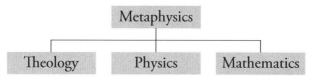

12. The first of these three sciences, theology, also called "divinity," deals with the nature of incorporeal things that do not belong to bodies, such as God and all divine matters. The second science, i.e., physics,[54] is concerned with the natures of corporeal things, such as animals and all the

things that have a body; from this science the art of medicine derived, so that, after the natures of man and of animals were known, together with the food, the herbs, and all the things that were suitable to them, the learned were able to define what health was and consequently could cure diseases. The object of the third science, mathematics, concerns the natures of incorporeal things which have to do with bodies. There being four of them, it is appropriate that mathematics should be divided into four branches, namely arithmetic, music, geometry, and astronomy,[55] as it appears from the following diagram:

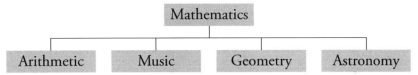

13. The first science, arithmetic, deals with counting and numbers, like the abacus and things at a deeper level. The second science, i.e., music, is about the harmonizing of voices and sounds. The third, geometry, concerns measurements and proportions. The fourth, astronomy, deals with the disposition of the sky and the stars. 14. Now the Commentator of this book turns to the first partition of philosophy, which has hitherto been neglected, and proposes to tell what is needed about the first part, namely, practice, in order to be able to discuss glorious rhetoric. As has been said before, practice is the science which shows what has to be done and what should be avoided; this it does in three ways which correspond to three different sciences, namely, ethics, economics, and politics,[56] as is shown by the following diagram:

15. The first, ethics, is the science of good and honest life and teaches us how to recognize what is honorable and useful and what is not, which it does by instructing us in four virtues, namely, prudence, justice, fortitude, and temperance, as well as by forbidding us to pursue such vices as pride, envy, wrath, avarice, gluttony, and lust. In this way, ethics shows what is to be pursued and what to be avoided to lead a virtuous life. 16. The second science, economics, shows what must be done and what must be avoided in order to protect our family and watch over our personal possessions. 17. The third science, i.e., politics, deals with the ruling over states and

Communes and, as has been said before, can be practiced in two ways, by deeds and by words,[57] as the following diagram shows:

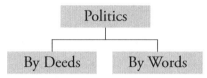

18. "Deeds" include all the arts and crafts that are practiced in cities by, e.g., smiths, drapers, and other craftsmen without whom cities could not survive. "Words" concern what can be done by language alone and includes three sciences, grammar, dialectics, rhetoric,[58] according to the following diagram:

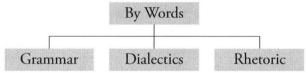

19. The proof that this is true—the Commentator says—lies in the fact that grammar is the beginning and the basis of all the liberal arts. It teaches how to speak and write correctly in appropriate words, without barbarisms or solecisms.[59] Certainly, without grammar nobody could speak well and write letters correctly. The second science, i.e., dialectics, proves what is said by means of arguments that demonstrate the truth of the words that have been spoken; certainly whoever wishes to speak and write letters appropriately should be able to prove what he says, so that those who listen can believe him and trust his words. The third science, that is, rhetoric, finds and adorns words that are suitable to the subject, so that whoever listens is pacified, believes what he has heard, is satisfied, and inclined to act according to what has been said. 20. Therefore, the three sciences are necessary to speaking and to the writing of letters, without which these activities would amount to nothing, since the good speaker or letter writer must speak and write so correctly and in such appropriate words so as to make himself understood, and this is the task of grammar; he further must demonstrate and give reasons for what he says, and this is what dialectics is for; he finally must organize and embellish his speech in order to be believed by those who listen to him, who must be satisfied with what he says and persuaded to do as he thinks fit, and this is fulfilled by rhetoric. 21. Now the Commentator maintains that that part of the science of politics which, in the ruling of cities, depends on eloquence is of two

kinds: one implies controversy and the other does not.[60] The first involves questions and answers according to the rules of dialectics, rhetoric, and law; the other also involves questions and answers, but its aim, instead of controversy, is to teach people how to act well, as it occurs in the works of the poets who have committed to paper the ancient stories, the great battles, and all the events which move people's minds to good actions. 22. That part of the science of politics which involves controversy is also of two kinds: one is artificial[61] while the other is not. It is artificial whenever the speaker, well acquainted with the nature and the state of the question, adds appropriate arguments according to the rules of dialectics and rhetoric. The non-artificial one derives its arguments from some authority, e.g., the law, not from demonstrations or reasons but only from the authority of the ruler who established it. Of this Boethius in his *Topics* says that it is without art and without argument.[62] 23. Eventually Tullius concludes that rhetoric is part of the science of politics. Victorinus, however, commenting on that definition, states that rhetoric is the greatest part of the science of politics, and "greatest" suggests the power of rhetoric to move mobs, parliaments, father against son, friend against friend, only to bring them to peace and good will once more.[63] After dealing with the genus, Tullius will now turn to the task and the aim of rhetoric.

18. Tullius Explains What Is the Task of This Art

1. The task of this art appears to be to speak appropriately in order to persuade; its aim is to persuade by means of words. There is a difference between "task" and "aim," in that the task takes into consideration what is suitable to the aim, while the aim pursues what is suitable to the task. Just as we consider the physician's task to treat in order to heal, and his aim to heal by means of drugs, in the same way what we call the task of rhetoric is what the rhetorician must do, while his aim is what he uses rhetoric for.

18. The Commentator

1. In this section Tullius has defined the task and the aim of rhetoric. As the text is very clear, the Commentator will only briefly deal with it. And he gives the following definitions: the task of rhetoric is to speak appropriately in order to persuade; by "appropriately," he emphasizes the fact that the rhetorician's words should be adorned with fine counsel according to the rules of the art. This Tullius says in order to distinguish this kind of speech

from that of the grammarians, who do not care to use ornate words. He also says "to persuade," that is, to speak so appropriately that those who listen are inclined to believe what is being said. This he says to distinguish that kind of speech from that of the poets, who are more interested in finding fine words than in persuading the audience. 2. The other definition concerns the aim of rhetoric: he says that it consists in the art of persuading through words. Certainly, whoever thinks of the aim of this art will admit that the rhetorician's only end is to make the audience believe his words. Therefore, this is the aim: to persuade; for, once a man believes what has been said, he immediately makes up his mind to share the rhetorician's wishes and act accordingly. 3. Moreover, Boethius in the fourth book of *Topics*[64] maintains that the aim of this art is twofold: one concerns the rhetorician and the other the audience. The rhetorician wishes to fulfil the aim in itself, i.e., to speak well and be thought by his audience to have spoken well; the aim of the audience is to be certain that the speaker's end is to persuade those who listen to him—and this is not every rhetorician's aim, as has been said before. 4. Therefore, in order to define the task and the aim more clearly, as well as the differences between them, Tullius says that the task is what the rhetorician should do when speaking according to the rules of the art, while the aim is the reason why he delivers his speech appropriately, both functions certainly aiming at nothing else but persuading people of what is being said. He gives the example of the physician whose task is to treat his patient appropriately in order to cure him, while his aim is to heal the patient by his treatment. 5. Now, after discussing the task and the aim exhaustively, in what follows the subject matter of rhetoric will be taken into account.

19. About the Subject Matter of Rhetoric

1. By subject matter of this art we intend whatever can be included in the art itself, as well as in the knowledge it produces. Just as we say that diseases and wounds are the physician's matter, since all medicine has to do with them, in the same way we call the matter of rhetoric the subjects this art is concerned with and the knowledge that derives from it; some believe there are more possible subjects, while others think that there are fewer. For example, Gorgias of Lentini, probably the first rhetorician of all, believed that the orator can speak very well about anything. Therefore, he appears to give this art a very ample and almost unlimited subject matter. However, Aristotle, who greatly improved and refined this art, maintained that the orator's task concerns three kinds of things: namely, the demonstrative, the deliberative, and the judicial.

19. The Commentator

1. In this section Tullius states that the subject matter of rhetoric is any thing because of which the rules of the art were conceived and devised, and because of which the science acquired by means of these rules operates. In the same way, the laws of medicine were discovered, as well as the treatment of diseases and wounds. In conclusion, this is the subject matter on which it is convenient to speak, and this is the reason why the art of rhetoric was devised, i.e., to teach eloquence according to the requirements of the subject as well as to persuade the audience. 2. Differences of opinion arose among the learned people, since many believed that the subject matter of eloquence could be anything one can speak about. If this were true, the art would have no limit, which is impossible. Among these was a very learned man, Gorgias of Lentini, a very ancient rhetorician;[65] but the very fact that Tullius says he was very ancient shows that he is not to be relied upon. 3. But Aristotle, who is absolutely trustworthy and greatly improved and refined this art, since he wrote a book on invention and another on speech, claims that rhetoric concerns three kinds of subject matters, each being a genus with its subdivisions,[66] and these are the demonstrative, the deliberative, and the judicial, as is shown in the diagram below:

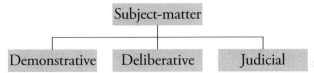

This being also Tullius's opinion, it can be concluded that the art of rhetoric consists of these three sorts of things. 4. But the masters of this art may at this point well make a distinction between eloquence and letter writing; for the concern of letter writing appears to be so general that letters can be written about almost anything, while the same is not true of rhetoric, which can only be concerned with one of the three above-mentioned subject matters. Therefore, Tullius defines all rhetoric as a disputation in words; by disputation, I mean a statement where words are so entangled that they can support one part or another, that is, they can demonstrate the pros and the cons by discussing the features of a person or of a fact. 5. By way of example, here is a question that could be asked in this way: "Should Marcus Tullius Cicero be exiled or not? For he ordered many Roman citizens to be killed[68] before the Roman people when the Commune itself was unsafe?" There are two possible answers to this question, one affirmative and the other negative. The affirmative one argues: Cicero is to be banished because he actually did such a thing; the negative says he should not be exiled because his name has a good record, while to be banished and exiled is certainly bad, and is it impossible to believe that a good man may act in such a way as to deserve banishment and exile. 6. The subject matter of this art has already been defined, and Tullius endorses Aristotle's opinion, and, since he has endorsed it, he will discuss exhaustively the three matters that have been mentioned in order to make the person to whom the book is addressed understand, through the words of Tullius and of the Commentator, the subject, the progress, and the nature of rhetoric. But first let him endeavor to fully grasp the subject and the contents of this book, otherwise it would be impossible for him to understand what follows; therefore, we shall begin with the demonstrative genus.

20. Of Demonstration

1. Demonstrative is called any argument in praise or blame of a certain person.

20. The Commentator

1. In this section Tullius explains that, given that there are three kinds of cases and disputations that occur whenever one is in favor and another against a controversial matter, he will first deal with the demonstrative one. The Commentator, however, will not proceed before he has defined the nature and the origin of all three of them, beyond what Tullius says; he will therefore explain who the orator is in the discussion of a case, and what the subject matter of the case is. 2. The orator is the person involved in a controversy because of something he said or did, that is, because of something he actually said, or is reasonably believed to have said, even if he did not say that at all; in the same way, "did" refers to something he really did or is reasonably supposed to have done, even if he did not actually do it. 3. The matter of the case is whatever has been said or done that starts a controversy or a quarrel. By way of example: suppose Pompey says to Catiline: "You are a traitor of the city of Rome"; and let Catiline answer: "No, I am not."[69] In this situation Pompey and Catiline are the contenders, and the case is: "You are a traitor," "No, I am not"; it is called a case because one speaks against the other, and thus a quarrel arises. 4. For the sake of clarity, the Commentator will define demonstration, deliberation, and judgment, that is, all the possible kinds of rhetoric.

Demonstration

5. A demonstration is a kind of case where the orator shows whether something is honorable or dishonorable, and therefore what is to be praised and what blamed. This kind of case is twofold: one is theoretical and general,[70] while the other cannot be shared by many people and therefore concerns individuals. 6. In the theoretical and general one, orators endeavor to show that something is honorable or dishonorable without mentioning any specific person; by "specific person," I mean an individual man, a city, a battle, and everything that concerns people, certainly not the height of the sky, the dimensions of the sun or the moon, these being matters not pertaining to the realm of rhetoric. 7. An example of such a demonstrative case is the following statement: "the strong man is to be praised," while the opponent maintains: "No, he is to be blamed," from which the controversy arises whether a strong man is to be praised or blamed; from this point of view, the controversy is a demonstrative one, and it is general since it does not mention any specific person. 8. The object of the individual demonstrative case concerns what is honorable or dishonorable with respect to a well-defined person whose name is explicitly mentioned, such as: "Marcus Tullius Cicero is praiseworthy," while the opponent says: "No, he is not," wherefrom the controversy arises whether he is to be praised or blamed. The question may refer to two different periods: present and past, that is to say the object of praise or blame can be either what the man is doing at the moment or what he did in the past. 9. This we find in the ancient Roman records where we learn that this kind of demonstrative case was discussed in the Campo Marzio, where people assembled to praise those who deserved position and power, and blame those who were unworthy of them.[71] This is all there is to be said about the demonstrative case. The Master will now deal with the deliberative one.

21. Of Deliberation

1. Deliberative can be defined as anything that, having become the object of a civil debate and query among citizens, finds a solution in the expression of a judgment.

21. The Commentator

1. In this section Tullius defines a deliberative case as one which is posed and given to citizens to debate among themselves in order to learn how they feel about it. Many opinions are obtained from this practice, so that

ultimately the best can be chosen. 2. This method is constantly used by rulers and statesmen[72] when they summon their counselors to decide what should be done about a certain matter and what avoided; then almost everyone gives an opinion, and the one which appears to be the best is chosen. 3. For instance, let a senator ask: "Should an army be sent to Macedonia?"[73] One is in favor, another against it. They decide which is the better course to take and choose it. This applies also to future events, since man is actually called upon thinking about future matters and deciding about them, i.e., whether something should be done or not. 4. Moreover, this deliberative case is a twofold one: one theoretical and general, and the other related to individuals. 5. The theoretical one is concerned with the general question about whether something is helpful or harmful, without any reference to individual beings. For example, should anyone say "Peace is to be kept among the Christians," while the opponent argues "It is not"; from this a general deliberative case arises whether peace should be kept or not. 6. The individual one occurs when the orators endeavor to prove whether something is helpful or harmful by explicit mention of individuals, as it occurs if one says: "Peace should be kept between the citizens of Milan and of Cremona,"[74] while the opponent argues: "It should not." 7. So much for the deliberative case. Now the judicial will be dealt with. It is, however, important to emphasize that the main feature of the deliberative case is to show what is helpful and what is harmful in a certain situation. This kind of case used to be discussed in the Senate: first, the counselors decided among themselves whether something was helpful or not, then their opinion was brought before the Parliament, where their decision was accepted or, perhaps, a different and better course was taken.

22. About the Judicial Case

1. Judicial is any question that is discussed in a law court and consists of either an accusation and a defense, or of a petition and a refutation.

22. The Commentator

1. The nature of a judgment implies a kind of discourse where the orator's aim is to show the justice or injustice of something, that is, whether something conforms to justice or is against it. It occurs as follows: somebody accuses one of something, and the accused defends himself or is defended by somebody else; or, perhaps someone places a petition asking for a reward for something he has done well, while the other refuses it, arguing that he

is not to be rewarded, and he can even say: "On the contrary, this is to be blamed." 2. Therefore, a legal suit arises, and it is tried in court, before the judges, so that they can decide who is right; this is done in open court, in a public session, so that the punishment given to evildoers can set an example for people not to do evil, and the reward given to those who behave well can set an example for others to do well. About this, a wise man said: good people avoid sin for the love of virtue, the bad ones for fear of punishment.[75] 3. This judicial case is twofold: one is theoretical and general, while the other is related to individuals. In the theoretical one, the orator endeavors to show whether something is right or wrong without mentioning any individual being, as it occurs in the following example: "a thief is to be hanged when he commits a theft"; the opponent says: "He is not." 4. In the individual one, the orator tries to prove the justice or injustice of a fact by explicit mention of an individual, for instance: "Is Guy to be hanged because he committed a theft?" Or, perhaps: "Is Julius Caesar to be rewarded for having conquered France, or not?"[76] 5. All judicial cases concern the past, since one is punished or rewarded for something he has done.

23. Tullius Gives His Opinion on Rhetoric and Discusses the Theory of Hermagoras

1. In our opinion, therefore, the art and science of eloquence consists of this threefold material. Hermagoras, however, does not seem to understand what he says, nor to fulfil what he has promised, since he divides the subject matter of this art into cases and questions.[77]

23. The Commentator

1. Having discussed the threefold nature of the subject matter of rhetoric according to Aristotle's classification,[78] Tullius now confirms Aristotle's theory and gives his own views on the subject by analyzing the opinion of Hermagoras, who thought the subject matter of rhetoric to be twofold, that is, to consist of cases and questions. 2. He did this in order to blame those who used to add to the subject matter of this art persuasion, dissuasion, and consolation, and Tullius blames him by mentioning his name directly since he came after many others and should have been subtler; he also criticizes him since his conclusions seem to be far-fetched with respect to the nature of the art, and in criticizing him, he also appears to blame the others. But since Tullius does not explicitly express his criticism of the other people, the Commentator will clearly show their failure in what

follows: 3. It is true, and has been demonstrated before, that the orator's task is to speak in order to persuade; this concerns mainly matters that are the subject of controversies not yet definitely contemplated in the mind. But if one really thinks about it, he will find that persuasion and dissuasion can only concern what the mind has already acquired. For example: the Commentator had planned to write this book, but he was not seriously working at it because of his negligence, which he was ultimately able to overcome through somebody's persuasion; such persuasion acted on something that was already present in his mind, namely, negligence. 4. If someone is discouraged from doing evil so that he actually avoids doing it, such dissuasion concerns an action which must be already firm in his mind. This proves that persuasion and dissuasion cannot be the subject matters of the art of rhetoric. 5. However, consolation can be material for the orator, in that it may concern something which is not yet in somebody's mind. For example, one man had resolved in his heart to lead a mournful life after the death of a person he loved above everything else. A wise man comforted him and even urged him to be merry, a feeling that had not yet reached the unhappy man's mind. However, in this behavior there is no controversy because the man who is comforted does not defend himself, nor does he argue against the person who is trying to comfort him; therefore, consolation cannot be material for rhetoric. 6. It is true that other people believed demonstration to be material not of rhetoric but of poetry, since it is a poet's task to praise or blame other people. Although Tullius does not blame them individually, the fact that he says that he agrees with Aristotle that demonstration, deliberation, and judgment are the subject matters of this art is enough to gather that he really blames them.[79] 7. Moreover, he remarks that demonstration concerns both orators and poets, but in different ways, for poets praise or blame without controversy, having no opponents, while the orator's praise or blame involves a controversy, since there are those who argue against him. Therefore, Tullius says that Hermagoras seemed not to understand what he stated, nor to consider what he promised, when he maintained that all cases and questions can be solved by means of rhetoric. Now Tullius will explain where he disagrees with Hermagoras about cases and questions.

24. Tullius Agrees with Hemagoras on the Definition of "Case," etc.

1. A case occurs whenever there is a controversy which is the object of an oration that involves individuals; this—we agree—belongs to the art

of rhetoric and, as has been said before, consists of three parts: judicial, demonstrative, and deliberative.

24. The Commentator

1. After arguing that Hermagoras did not fully understand what he was saying when he stated that cases and questions are the subject matters of the science of rhetoric, in this section Tullius analyzes Hermagoras's definition of a case. 2. A "case" he calls a subject on which there is disagreement among some people, one being of one opinion, while another being of a different one. A verbal contention therefore arises, and this involves a person, a well-known individual, and nobody else who is professionally and technically concerned with civil matters. 3. In this—Tullius says—he agrees with Hermagoras because of the opinion he has formed by himself and because of Aristotle's authority. He will now explain where Hermagoras went wrong when he defined a question.

25. Here Tullius Disagrees with Hermagoras

1. A question is defined as a controversy involving a speech where no individual is involved. For example: "Is there any good beyond honesty?" "Are the senses to be trusted?" "What is the shape of the world?" "What are the dimensions of the sun?" We easily understand that all these questions are far from the orator's concern, for there is great madness and foolishness in asking the orator to solve, as if they were trifles, these questions that have engaged, with the greatest labor, the minds of the philosophers.

25. The Commentator

1. Here Tullius explains that Hermagoras called a question something many people disagreed about, so that there was a lively verbal contention among them, but no person professionally involved in civil matters was mentioned. 2. The following example is given: "Is there any good beyond honesty?" There was a great controversy among philosophers as to what was the supreme good in life; many said it was honesty, and these were the Peripatetic; others thought it was will, and these were the Epicureans.[80] 3. Another question was whether the senses can be trusted or not, since they sometimes deceive us; for instance, when we believe brass to be gold, our senses are certainly mistaken. 4. Then, there was the problem of the shape of the world, which some philosophers showed to be round, while others believed to be elliptical, octagonal, or square. 5. The dimensions of the sun were also debated, some

maintaining it is eight times bigger than the earth, while others argued that it is less than that, and others more. These dimensions were the object of many measurements on the part of the ancient masters of geometry, who tried to elicit them from their measurements of the Earth. 6. Therefore, Tullius shows that Hermagoras did not understand what he was talking about, since it is easily demonstrated that such questions do not concern the orator's task; mind that he says "task," since the orator might well be a philosopher, and in that case he would certainly have to be concerned with those problems, but that would not be in his capacity as an orator but as a philosopher. So he is certainly out of his mind and foolish enough who claims that the rhetorician may, or even has to, deal with those matters that are the philosophers' arduous and time-consuming activity. 7. After showing that Hermagoras did not really understand what he was saying, Tullius will show he did not fulfil what he had promised when he proclaimed he would deal with every case and question by means of rhetoric. 8. In fact, he did as some learned people do when, wishing to show their learning, they apply it to an art by which it cannot be proved, as if one, to discuss a question of dialectics, dealt with it as if it were one of grammar, through which it cannot nor could be proved; but they believe that arguing about it shows their learning. Here is what Tullius says of these matters.

26. Tullius Summarizes What He Has Said Before

1. If Hermagoras, by studying and learning, had acquired a great knowledge of these matters, he would appear to have established through his learning a false principle of the art of the orator, in order to show not what this art can do but what he himself was capable of. But Hermagoras is a man of so great ability that one would sooner deny him acquaintance with rhetoric than admit his knowledge of philosophy. However, his art does not seem to me completely worthless, since he appears to have placed in it some ideas skilfully and diligently taken from ancient works not without some original additions of his own; but it is no great enterprise to talk about the art as he did, while it is a much greater feat to speak according to its principles, which we see he was unable to do. Therefore, we believe the subject matter of rhetoric to be the one indicated by Aristotle, which we have already discussed.

26. The Commentator

1. In this section Tullius says that even if Hermagoras had been so wise as to be able to deal with cases and questions, he would apparently have been

wrong in assigning the orator a task not his own, thereby not showing the power of that art, but only his own skill. 2. "But Hermagoras is a man of so great ability," means that he was such a man that nobody who claimed he was not well acquainted with rhetoric would have thought him to be a philosopher. 3. "His art does not seem to me to be completely worthless." By this expression, Tullius defends him and shows he could have done much worse. "Not completely worthless" means that he put in his book some ideas skilfully and diligently chosen from other authorities of this art, and even added something new. Here Tullius appears to be praising him where he is instead blaming him, since he accuses him of having been a thief in making up his book with other masters' writings. 4. "But it is no great enterprise to talk about the art" means that it is not the orator's task to establish the rules of rhetoric, as Hermagoras did, but to speak according to its teachings and principles, which he was incapable of doing.[81] 5. We should therefore follow Aristotle[82] who claims the subject matter of this art to be demonstration, deliberation, and judgment. The genus, the task, and the end of rhetoric having now exhaustively and diligently been dealt with, we turn to the discussion of its parts, as Tullius has promised earlier in his book.

27. Tullius on the Parts of Rhetoric

1. The parts of rhetoric are generally understood to be *inventio, dispositio, elocutio, memoria,* and *pronuntiatio.*[83]

27. The Commentator

1. Tullius claims rhetoric to consist of five parts, and explains why; the Commentator will analyze them one by one in due course. But first he will discuss the reasons given by Boethius in the fourth book of his *Topica,* where he says that if one of these parts is missing, the oration is not complete; on the other hand, if these parts are in an oration or in a letter, then certainly rhetoric is there, as well. 2. Boethius gives also another reason: these parts belong to rhetoric since they give it shape and structure and make it what it is, exactly as the foundations, the walls, and the roof are parts of a house, so that it exists as such and would not be complete should any of these parts be missing.[84] Therefore, Tullius says that these are the parts of rhetoric according to the general understanding, since there were some who claimed that *memoria* is not part of rhetoric because it is not a science, while others excluded *dispositio* from the features of this

art. 3. Tullius will therefore proceed to discuss all of them beginning with invention, the worthiest of all, which it really is, since it can exist without the others, while they cannot exist without it.

28. Tullius on Invention

1. *Inventio* consists of endeavoring to find truthful or plausible arguments in order to prove one's case.

28. The Commentator

1. Tullius defines *inventio* as the science by means of which we find truthful issues, that is, necessary arguments—"necessary," namely, that cannot be but as they are—and plausible ones, that is, arguments suitable to prove that what we said is true, by means of which true and plausible arguments what somebody has said or done, in his own defense or against another person, can be proved or made credible. 2. And this the Commentator's friend, whom he calls his "harbor,"[85] can interpret as follows. For example: let a case occur where one should speak either in defense of someone or against another person, or, perhaps, imagine that the subject must be dealt with by letter. In this case, neither the tongue should be let loose nor the hand should rush to put pen to paper; the wise man, instead, carefully weighs his words before he ever begins to speak or write. In the same way, a good architect and master builder, once he has planned to build a house, before setting to work, turns over in his mind what the house is going to be like and how he can make it in the best possible way. Only after he has made up his mind about all that, does he begin to work.[86] The same applies to the good rhetorician: he should carefully think about the nature of the case he is going to deal with and find true or plausible arguments suitable to it, so as to prove them and make what he says credible. 3. So much for *inventio*. We now turn to *dispositio*.

29. Tullius on *Dispositio*

1. *Dipositio* is a careful arrangement of what has been found.

29. The Commentator

1. Since the finding of arguments to prove what has been said or make it credible is worth nothing unless they are arranged in the proper order, that is, unless each argument is placed in the convenient part or position, so that the orator's opinion is emphasized, Tullius discusses *dispositio*. 2. He

defines it as the science that allows us to arrange the arguments we have found in the appropriate order, that is, the stronger ones at the beginning, the weaker in the middle, and the most forcible ones, that cannot easily be opposed, at the end. 3. This is what the architect of a house does: after he has planned the building in his mind, he sets the foundations in a convenient place and then proceeds with the walls, the roof, the entrance, the rooms, and passages, and to each he assigns its appropriate collocation. After defining *dispositio*, *elocutio* will be dealt with.

30. Tullius on *Style*

1. *Elocutio* is a choice of words and expressions suitable to *inventio*.

30. The Commentator

1. Since finding and arranging words without being able to adorn one's discourse with pleasant words and good counsel, suitable to the subject, is worth nothing, Tullius defines *elocutio* as the science of adding adornment of words and expressions to what has been found and properly arranged. 2. He further remarks that an adornment of words is a sort of dignity which originates in some of the words in the oration and makes the whole speech shine through. For example: "The great virtue that prevails in you encourages me to hope in your help." The word "prevails" certainly casts light on all the other words in the sentence. 3. In the same way, adornment is a quality of the chosen expressions that comes from the way they are elegantly joined to each other in a speech. Let us, for instance, consider the following words pronounced by Solomon: "The wounds inflicted by a friend are sweeter than an enemy's deceitful kisses."[87] 4. In this way, *elocutio*, that is, an arrangement of words and expressions capable of making an oration pleasant and well organized, has been discussed. Tullius now turns to the fourth part of rhetoric, namely, *memoria*.

31. Tullius on *Memory*

31. "Memory" is a firm grasp within the mind of concepts, words, and of their arrangement.

31. The Commentator

1. Since finding, arranging, and adorning words without keeping them in the memory, so that we can recall them when speaking or writing letters, is

worth nothing, Tullius defines memory and says that it is twofold, natural and artificial.[88] 2. The natural one is a power of the mind that allows us to remember what we have learnt through any of the bodily senses. 3. The artificial one is a science which is acquired through the teachings of the philosophers and that allows us—once we have mastered them well—to remember what we have heard, found, or perceived through our bodily senses. It is the artificial memory—Tullius says—that is part of rhetoric.[89] He defines memory as the science by means of which we retain in our mind the things and the words we have found and arranged, so that we can recall them when we have to speak. After discussing memory, Tullius will now turn to the fifth and last part of rhetoric, that is, *pronuntiatio*.

32. Tullius on Delivery

1. *Pronuntiatio* can be defined as the bearing of the body and the tone of the voice which fit the dignity of the subject matter and of the words.

32. The Commentator

1. It is true that finding, arranging, adorning, and remembering words are of little worth unless one can deliver one's speech with the proper attitude. This is why at the end of his discussion, Tullius focuses on delivery and defines it as the science of uttering words, controlling and tuning one's voice, taking up the right bearing of body and limbs according to the nature of the event and the context of the speech. 2. For whoever really wants to speak truthfully should consider that the tone of the voice and the attitude of the body are different when pain rather than joy is the subject of the speech, and that the same applies to orations concerning peace rather than war. The orator wishing to move people to war must speak in a loud voice and use bold and brave words, show a proud bearing of the body, as well as a fierce countenance against the enemies. 3. And if his oration is to be delivered on horseback, the horse must be big and healthy, so that while the orator is speaking, his horse should neigh and scrape the ground with its paw, raise dust, and blow from its nostrils to the point that the whole place should be in turmoil as if the assault had started and the battle already begun.[90] At this point it may not seem inappropriate for the speaker to raise his hand from time to time in order to show his courage or appear to threaten the enemy. 4. On the contrary, if the subject is peace, the bodily attitude should be humble, the countenance friendly, the voice sweet, the words peaceful, the hands quiet. The horse should be calm,

meek, and so still that not a hair should move, so as to look the very image of peace. 5. In the same way, if the subject is a joyful one, let the orator's head be kept high, his countenance show gladness, and his whole attitude and words point to happiness. But if suffering is his subject, the orator's head should be bowed, his attitude sad, his eyes full of tears, so that his whole look and all his words should move the audience's souls to sadness and tears. 6. Now the five constituting parts of rhetoric have been defined entirely following Tullius's opinion, and the Commentator has done his best to explain them to his host.[91] Tullius apologizes again because he has not yet shown why the task, the genus, and the aim of rhetoric are the ones he has been dealing with, as he has done in the case of the subject matter and of its parts. He now proceeds as follows.

33. Tullius Promises to Deal with the Subject Matter of Rhetoric and Its Parts

1. After briefly describing these matters, the reasons why the genus, the task, and the aim of rhetoric can be defined as we have done will be discussed later, since they are lengthy to deal with and not so important to show the properties and the rules of the art. On the other hand, if one writes about the art of rhetoric, it is also convenient for him to write about the other two aspects, i.e., about its subject matter and its parts. Therefore, the subject matter of rhetoric and its parts will be discussed together. In doing this, in all kinds of cases *inventio* should be considered with the greatest attention, since she is the princess of all the parts of rhetoric.[92]

33. The Commentator

1. In this section Tullius explains that he prefers not to show why the one he has mentioned before is a genus of rhetoric or to discuss the tasks and aims of this art, since this would take a very long time and would not be very helpful; he will therefore deal with these subjects in the other book, which is entirely devoted to them.[93] In the present one he will deal with the subject matter of rhetoric, i.e., demonstration, deliberation, and judgment, as well as with its parts, namely, *inventio*, *dispositio*, *elocutio*, *memoria*, and *pronuntiatio*. 2. All these will be dealt with together and at the same time. *Inventio* being the most important part of the oration, Tullius maintains that it must be present in all genera of rhetoric, since finding arguments is essential whether the subject matter is a demonstrative case, a deliberative,

or a judicial one. He will show at the same time how the subject matter can be found in each case, how it should be arranged and embellished, and how the oration can be memorized and eventually delivered.

The Commentator Speaks to His Friend

3. Therefore, the Commentator asks his host,[94] since he himself has engaged in such a big enterprise, to be pleased to give his whole mind to what has been said before, in order to become acquainted with the demonstrative, the deliberative, and the judicial kinds of oration that are the foundations of the whole art of rhetoric; he should then become acquainted with what follows in this treatise, so that his full learning and the eloquence he will display according to the rules of the art will give the book and its Commentator eternal glory.

34. About the Issue and Its Four Parts

1. Every subject involving a verbal controversy or a debate has in itself a question of fact, of name, of genus, or of legal action. The question that starts the whole case is called the "issue."[95] The issue is the source of disagreement in a case, arising from the controversy about an accusation, such as "You did it," "I did not do it," or, perhaps, "I was right in doing it."

34. The Commentator

1. Since Tullius has decided to deal with invention and subject matter at the same time, the Commentator will show the order in which he discusses *inventio*; for the sake of clarity, however, he will first explain the meaning of such words as "case," "controversy," "issue," and "status." 2. The case is any thing somebody said or did that started the controversy; the name "case" is given to the whole proceedings and concerns both parties. "Case" refers to the whole oration and contention, from the prologue to the conclusion; therefore, one can say "My case is right," meaning, "I am on the right side." 3. "Controversy" is much the same as case, and implies the use of different and opposite arguments with respect to those of the opponent. 4. A question is the first argument of the person who brings the charge against the opponent, as well as the answering speech of the person who defends himself. A question is therefore an oration where the two contenders express their arguments under the form of doubts, and the name applies to statement and rejoinder alike. 5. The issue has already

been defined. 6. Status is what the opponent said and did and which the orators endeavor to demonstrate. This is also called an issue, since the orator establishes[96] and arranges his arguments and decides his position about what was said or done. It is also called a controversy, since different people have a different understanding of it.

Here the Commentator Shows How Tullius Is Going to Discuss Invention

7. After the Commentator has explained the meaning of these words, he will show in what order Tullius deals with invention. And certainly he first shows how to look for, and find, the matters orators are concerned with, and calls them issues, the properties, and parts of which he illustrates. 8. Secondly, he shows what cases are simple, i.e., made up of two parts only, and what are composite, i.e., made up of four parts or more. 9. Thirdly, he distinguishes between written and spoken controversies. 10. In the fourth place, he shows those things that arise from an issue, that is, the oration, which has two parts and sources, as well as the verdict and the defender's argument. 11. In the fifth place, Cicero shows how the parts of an oration should be dealt with according to rhetoric. 12. In the sixth place, he shows the number and the nature of these parts, and the way to handle each of them. 13. In conclusion, Tullius's text is arranged in such a way as to show the origin of all the matters that concern an orator.

The Commentator

14. Any thing involving a controversy, that is, something about which different people feel in different ways, so that they speak about it inquisitively, in order to learn whether one of the parties is true or false, is called an "issue of fact," as it originates in a deed one is accused of. For example, let one accuse another man: "You set fire to the Capitol," and let the other answer "I did not."[97] So the issue is whether the accused did it or not, and it is named an issue of fact because of the deed the man is charged with. 15. In a definitional issue, instead, one part defines a deed in a certain way, and the other in a different one. For instance, suppose someone steals a horse from a church or, in any case, something that is not considered a sacred object. So one accuses him "You committed a sacrilege," while the other remarks, "Not a sacrilege, but a theft."[98] Now, a sacrilege is a much more serious crime than a theft, since it consists of stealing a sacred object from a sacred place. A controversy, therefore, arises concerning the name

that should be given to the crime, whether sacrilege or theft, and this is called a "definitional issue." 16. There may also be a question of the nature of a deed, that is, of the quality of an action, when one party considers a deed of a certain nature and the other believes it to be of another one. For example, one says, "He was right in murdering his own mother, because she had murdered his father," while the other argues against that: "It is not true, he was not justified in doing it."[99] Therefore, a controversy arises concerning the nature of the deed, i.e., whether it was right or wrong, and this is called an "issue of genus," that is, one concerning the quality of the deed. 17. Sometimes, it can be a question of action, i.e., the issue may involve an action which is different according to the place or the time it was performed. For instance, let one accuse another person "You have stolen one of my horses," to which the accused answers: "It is true, but I am not going to justify myself now, because," say, "you are my servant"; or perhaps, "because it is a holiday"; or "the only right court for it is that of my country, not this one."[100] From this a controversy arises which, Tullius says, concerns the action, that is, whether the charge should be answered or not. 18. Tullius defines all the above-mentioned matters as "issues," and gives them this name. The issue—he states—is whatever starts a controversy in a case, i.e., what orators first argue about, the subject matter of their orations, and the source of the controversial debate between the accuser and the accused. 19. Therefore, the charge is the first speech of the accuser, while the first speech of the defender is called the "contention." The origin of the issue appears to be found in the contention to the charge, not because it really arises from it, but because from the defender's words it is possible to learn whether the controversy or the question concerns the deed, the type, the name, or the action, as is shown in the examples given above. 20. Tullius will now discuss the names, the divisions, the properties, and the motives of all the above-mentioned questions.

35. Of the Issue of Fact, Also Called "Conjectural"

1. Whenever the controversy concerns a fact, since the case is established by conjectures, it is named a "conjectural issue."

35. The Commentator

1. In this section Tullius explains that whenever the controversy concerns a deed someone is accused of, as has been said before, it must be solved by conjectures, that is, by assumptions and presumptions. For example,

suppose one accuses another man: "You did kill Ajax: I saw you take the knife out of his body."[101] 2. This is an arduous question, and, as Victorinus says, orators are usually in great difficulties when they try to prove something of this kind, since equally sound reasons can be produced in favour of both parts.[102] After discussing the conjectural issue, Tullius will deal with the issue called "definitional."

36. About the Name, i.e., the Definition, of an Issue

1. Whenever the controversy is about a name, since the power of a word is defined by means of other words, the issue is called "definitional."

36. The Commentator

1. In this part Tullius explains that when the controversy is about the name of a deed, that is, about the way the action someone is charged with should be called, the issue concerns the definition, since the power—that is, the meaning of that specific word or name—must be defined, i.e., explained and clarified, not by means of examples but by words that are concise, clear, and easy to grasp. 2. For instance, suppose a man, accused of having stolen a chalice from a consecrated place, and, therefore, charged with sacrilege, defends himself by arguing that his crime is not a sacrilege but a mere theft. The whole controversy is about the name of the deed: is it theft or sacrilege?[103] 3. Therefore, in order to arrive at the truth, both words must be defined, that is, the meaning and the sense of the words must be given; only after the meanings of the names have been made clear by means of other words, will it be possible to understand and decide which of the them applies to the deed in question. After discussing the name, Tullius will deal with the nature of a fact.

37. Tullius on the Nature of a Fact, That Is, on the General Issue

1. Whenever the nature of a fact is the subject of a debate, so that the controversy is about the importance and the kind of the fact, we speak of a general issue.

37. The Commentator

1. In this section Tullius explains that when the nature of a fact is debated, so that the controversy involves the importance of a deed, that is, its

quantity and its relationship to other facts, as well as its quality and kind, the issue is called "general." 2. For example, the quantity of the fact implies a discussion of the following question: whether one person did as much as another, e.g., whether Tullius had been of service to the Commune of Rome as much as Cato.[104] 3. Comparison involves a debate concerning two alternatives, as it occurred when the Romans seized Carthage and discussed whether to destroy it or let it exist.[105] 4. The kind of a fact concerns its quality, as in the example given above, where the question was whether the accused was right or wrong in doing what he did.

38. Tullius on the Action Called Translative

1. Whenever the case appears not to have been started by the right person or seems to be directed against the wrong man, or perhaps not at the appropriate time, under the wrong legislation, against the wrong crime, or with the inappropriate punishment, that issue is called "translative," since it implies an action of transfer and requires a change.

38. The Commentator

1. In this section Tullius deals with the controversy that concerns an action which, when it is necessary and appropriate, must be changed, in part or completely, and is therefore called "translative" or "transferable."

There are seven possible cases, and these are discussed in the book:

2. The controversy is not started by the right person. For example, a schoolboy says to another: "You were too late for school," and the other answers: "I am not going to discuss this with you, as you have no right to accuse me; only the teacher can do that."

3. The charge is brought against the wrong person. For instance, a conspiracy was discovered in Rome, and the charge was brought against Julius Caesar, who answered: "Not against me should the action be brought, but against Catiline, who behaved in this way in the past and still behaves in the same way."[106]

4. The action is brought before the wrong court. For instance, a bishop was accused of simony before the king of Navarre, and he protested: "You are not accusing me before the right judge, for I have to answer only to the pope."[107]

5. The time chosen to bring the charge is the wrong one. For instance, one man accused of a crime on Easter day, answered: "I am not going to answer this now, since this is not the appropriate day for such dealings."[108]

6. The legislation is not the right one. For instance, a Roman citizen, who happened to be in Paris, wanted to sue a Frenchman according to the Roman law, but the Frenchman answered that he only acknowledged the French law, not the Roman one.[109]

7. The charge is a wrong one. For example, a eunuch was charged with the rape of a young girl; he said: "This is not the kind of crime I am going to defend myself from."[110]

8. The punishment requested is inappropriate. For instance, a man who had killed a cock was sentenced to death by beheading; he said: "This is not the right punishment for such a crime."[111]

9. All these questions are therefore translative, since they must be changed into different facts or conditions, sometimes completely, sometimes in part, as it appears from the examples above.

39. Tullius Maintains That, Unless at Least One of These Four Issues Is Present, There Can Be No Case

1. It is therefore evident that at least one of these issues must be present in all kinds of cases, for no controversy would arise if all of them were absent, and then no case would exist.

39. The Commentator

1. After showing the parts of the issue and explaining what their main features are and how they are called, Tullius proceeds to demonstrate that, unless at least one of these issues concerning either the fact, the name, the quality, or the translation of an action is present in the orators' speeches, there can be no controversy between the speakers, and the fact they discuss is not a case and does not concern the art of rhetoric, being neither demonstrative, nor deliberative nor judicial. 2. By this Tullius proves that all the aspects of the art are related to one another, so that any case—either demonstrative, deliberative, or judicial—is necessarily an issue of fact, of name, of quality, or of action, and vice versa, and any issue concerning fact, name, quality, or action is necessarily demonstrative, deliberative, or judicial, as well. Now Tullius will proceed to deal with each part separately.

40. About the Fact

1. A controversy about a fact can concern any time. The question, in fact, can refer to the past, as in the following example: "Did Ulysses kill Ajax or

not?" It can refer to the present: "Are the Fregellans well disposed toward the State of Rome?" It can refer to what is still to come: "If we do not destroy Carthage, will this prove good or bad to the Commune?"[112]

40. The Commentator

1. In this part Tullius argues that a controversy concerning a fact that is brought against someone, which is called a conjectural issue, as has been said before and proved by examples, can concern any time, i.e., the past, the present, and the future. 2. As far as the past is concerned, he gives the example of Ajax's death, which occurred as follows. During the siege of Troy, the worthy Achilles died, and after his death a great controversy arose between Ulysses and Ajax concerning his weapons. 3. According to the old stories, Ulysses was certainly the wisest among the Greeks and the best orator, so that, because of his great wisdom and eloquence, he was able to perform great deeds, which others were incapable of; therefore, he caused more harm to the Trojans by his wisdom than the whole Greek army by its weapons. At the end, it was evident that he had invented the trick of the horse by which Troy was betrayed and lost; however, in war he neither spent great energies, nor was he very brave. Nonetheless, he claimed a right to Achilles's arms, as he said he deserved them for his behavior during the war, because, etc. 4. Ajax, on the contrary, was a proud knight and a brave warrior, capable of performing great deeds, but certainly not very wise or [eloquent]. He had behaved bravely in that war and claimed the right to Achilles's arms, which, according to him, Ulysses did not deserve. 5. In the end, after the arms had been given to Ulysses, such a great envy ensued between them that they became mortal foes. Meanwhile, Ajax died and Ulysses was accused of his death, but he defended himself and rejected the charge. This issue of fact concerns the past, because it occurred a long time ago. 6. As far as the present is concerned, Tullius quotes the Fregellans,[113] whom Rome accused of being ill-disposed toward the Commune. They defended themselves by claiming they had a good and favorable disposition toward it. This is an example of an issue of fact concerning the present, the question being whether these people were at that time well-disposed or not. 7. As an example of future time Tullius cites the case of Carthage, one of the noblest and strongest cities in the world. It started a war against Rome, which in the end the Romans won, and the country was conquered; some wanted the city to be destroyed for the safety of Rome, others argued against this opinion, since they believed the existence of Carthage to be good for Rome. The issue evidently concerned the

future, as the question was whether Carthage should be destroyed or not. 8. After dealing with the controversy of fact, Tullius will turn to the issue of name, as follows.

41. About the Name

1. A controversy concerning the name occurs when the fact is admitted, but there is no agreement about the way it should be called. And this is conveniently defined as a controversy of name or of definition, since the fact is not questioned, but its nature is disputed, one calling it in one way and the other in a different one. Consequently, the fact must be defined in words and briefly described; for example, if a sacred object is stolen from a private place, the question arises whether the crime should be considered a theft or a sacrilege. In this case, both words, i.e., theft and sacrilege, should be defined in order to show that the crime must be called in a different way from the one claimed by the opponents.

41. The Commentator

1. In this section Tullius discusses the controversy concerning the name of a fact. Since the subject has exhaustively been dealt with before, the Commentator will discuss it only briefly, quickly analyzing the subject matter by means of the following example. 2. Let Robert accuse Walter of having stolen a sacred object used in religious functions, such as a chalice or something of the kind, from a private place, perhaps a house or another non-consecrated place. Suppose the accused admits the deed. The accuser says: "You committed a sacrilege." And the accused answers: "It was not a sacrilege, but a theft."[114] So they agree on the fact but not about its nature, that is, about the features that allow one to distinguish a theft from a sacrilege, since the accuser and the accused have different opinions on the matter, one claiming the action to be a sacrilege, the other a theft. 3. In this case, the orator arguing on this subject should provide a definition and state briefly what a sacrilege is and what can be called a theft in order to show that the fact cannot bear the name given by his opponent. After dealing with the issue of name, Tullius will discuss the genus, as follows.

42. About the Nature of a Controversy

1. A controversy about the nature of a deed occurs when there is no

question about the fact and its name, but the quantity, the manner, and the quality are controversial, e.g., whether it is right or wrong, useful or useless; that is, whenever the nature of a deed is called into question.

42. The Commentator

1. In this section Tullius discusses the genus of a deed, which has already been extensively dealt with, so that the Commentator will speak very briefly about it and only emphasize that a controversy is about the genus or the nature of a deed whenever the accused admits the fact and agrees with the accuser about its name but disagrees with him on the quantity, that is, whether it is great or small, serious or negligible. 2. For example, an important Roman citizen ran away when he should have chased enemies out of the Commune.[115] He was accused of having harmed the city and stained the dignity of Rome. The accused admitted the fact and agreed about its name. The accuser argued: "It was great harm," while the accused retorted "No, it was a small one." The controversy concerns the quantity, namely, whether the harm was small or great. 3. There may also be a controversy about the manner, when two options are compared, as in the example of Carthage discussed above, where the alternatives were whether it should be destroyed or spared. 4. Furthermore, there can be a controversy about the quality of a deed, as is evident in the example about Orestes, who was accused of the unjust murder of his mother. He protested that he had been right in killing her; in this case, the deed and its name are not questioned, and the controversy concerns the quality, i.e., whether he was justified or not in committing the murder. 5. Actually, Tullius does not give examples concerning the quantity or the comparison between facts, but only the quality, since this one is likely to occur much more frequently than the others. Therefore, he considers controversies concerning the nature of a deed to be all the cases where there is agreement about the fact and its name, but there is disagreement about the quality of the deed. 6. After giving his opinion on this matter, Tullius immediately proceeds to blame Hermagoras for his misunderstanding of the controversy concerning the nature of a deed.

43–47. About Hermagoras's Error

1. Hermagoras distinguishes four species in this genus: i.e., deliberative, demonstrative, judicial, and legal. His mistake should be blamed as not a small one, but we should not dwell on it too much in order not to make

people think that, by overlooking it, we repeat it uncritically, or by laying too much stress on it, give the impression that we neglect other theories. 2. If deliberation and demonstration are genera of cases, they cannot be species of any genus of case, for something can well be genus of one thing and species of another but cannot be both species and genus of the same thing. The deliberative and the demonstrative are certainly genera of cases. Therefore, either there are no genera of cases at all, or there is only the judicial one, or there are judicial, demonstrative, and deliberative cases. But to argue that there are no genera of cases, while at the same time maintaining—as Hermagoras does—that the cases are numerous, and give rules for them, is sheer madness. There cannot be one genus only, not even the judicial, since the deliberative and the demonstrative are different from each other, and both differ from the judicial, each having its own end to fulfil. Therefore, since all three are genera of cases, it follows that neither the deliberative nor demonstrative can be considered species of any genus of case. Hermagoras is therefore ill advised in stating that they are species of the general issue. 3. And if they cannot be considered species of the general issue, still less can they rightly be considered subdivisions of species of the case. In fact, an issue is part of a case, for it is not the case that must fit the issue, but the issue that must fit the case. But the demonstrative and the deliberative cannot be held as species of a genus of case, exactly because they are themselves genera, and in no way can they be considered species of it. 4. Moreover, if the issue and its parts are a defense against an accusation, whatever is not a defense cannot be an issue, nor part of an issue. Now, deliberation and demonstration are certainly not issues; therefore, if the issue and its parts are a defense against an accusation, demonstration and deliberation are neither issues nor parts of issues. But Hermagoras is pleased to consider the issue a defense; therefore, he must be pleased not to consider deliberative and demonstrative speeches issues or parts of issues. Equally absurd is his opinion that the issue is the first statement of the accuser and the first plea of the defendant, an idea that led to still more absurd statements. 5. Furthermore, a conjectural case, i.e., one of fact, cannot, in the same part of the same genus, be both conjectural and definitional, and a definitional case cannot at the same time, and according to the same classification, be both definitional and translative.[116] In conclusion, no issue or part of an issue can have its own power and that of another one, since each one is simply considered according to its nature; and if another is considered, the number of issues is doubled, but the force of each is not enhanced in any way. Indeed, the deliberative case, at the same time and from the same point of view, can have a conjectural, a general, a definitional, and a translative issue, sometimes one of them, sometimes more than one. So it can be neither an issue, nor part of it. The same applies to the demonstrative case. In conclusion, as we have argued, deliberation and demonstration are genera of cases, not parts of any issues.

43–47. The Commentator

1. In this section Tullius explains that, according to Hermagoras, the general controversy has four subsections, namely, deliberative, demonstrative, judicial, and legal. Tullius blames him thoroughly and gives many reasons to show clearly, by means of the dialectical method, how deeply Hermagoras is wrong. He proves that demonstration and deliberation are genera of cases, so that the cases are parts of them, and being genera of cases, that is what the whole cases consist of, they cannot be parts of them, since something cannot be at the same time whole and part of the same thing. 2. Therefore, by many reasons and sound arguments, Tullius concludes that Hermagoras is wrong, and gives his own opinion on the parts of the general issue, on the quantity, manner, and quality of a fact, as has been said before. And his argument begins as follows.

48. The Parts of a General Issue

1. This general issue seems to us to have two parts: judicial and legal.

48. The Commentator

1. After rejecting Hermagoras's opinion concerning the four parts of the general issue, Tullius states that according to him there are only two parts: namely, the ones called by Hermagoras judicial and legal. He then immediately proceeds to account for this opinion which is superior to that of Hermagoras and of all the others, and shows which is judicial and which legal:

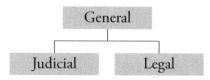

49. About the Judicial Issue

49. The judicial is the part of the general issue where the natures of right and equity are questioned, as well as the reasons for reward or punishment.

49. The Commentator

1. The judicial issue discusses a case in terms of justice, that is, according to the legislation established by habit or reasons of equity, following either the natural or the written law, the quantity, the relationship, or the quality of a deed in order to learn whether it is just, unjust, good, or evil. 2. Judicial can also be defined as the issue where it must be decided whether one should be rewarded or punished. For instance, is Alobroges worthy of praise for having disclosed Catiline's conspiracy?[117] The pros and the cons are discussed. Another example can also be given: Must Giraldus be punished since he committed a theft?[118] 3. After discussing the judicial issue, Tullius will now turn to the legal.

50. About the Legal Issue

1. Legal can be called the issue which discusses a fact according to the civil custom and according to justice, on which our law experts are called upon to give their opinions.

50. The Commentator

1. Tullius defines "legal" the issue where judgment is given, either according to the customs the citizens have developed in their habits and statutes, or according to equity, i.e., written laws. 2. Therefore, the difference between the judicial and the legal issue lies in the fact that the judicial deals with past things and time-honored written laws, while the legal is concerned with present and future matters, and involves the laws and habits which are to be written and developed. 3. This is a very hard enterprise, and the orators are fully engaged in endeavoring to test issues and find new statutes and customs by arguing in favor or against them. This issue is usually discussed before men who are both wise and competent in legal matters;[119] on the contrary, to prove a judicial issue it is sufficient to follow already established customs. 4. After Tullius has defined both the judicial and the legal issues, he will focus on the parts of the judicial in order to show the aim of each part of this art.

51. About the Two Parts of the Judicial Issue

1. The judicial issue is in turn divided into two parts: the absolute and the assumptive.

51. The Commentator

1. In this section Tullius explains that—as has been shown before—the issue which has been called "judicial" is composed of two parts: one called absolute, and the other assumptive. They will be discussed separately.

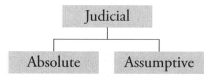

52. About the Absolute Issue

1. An absolute issue is one that has in itself the arguments for right or wrong doing.

52. The Commentator

1. Tullius says that the judicial issue is called "absolute" whenever it is free[120] and self-consistent, since it contains in itself, without any addition, all the arguments concerning the quality, the quantity, and the relationship between facts, so that it can be established whether a deed is profitable or harmful, right or wrong, good or evil, as the following example shows. 2. Were the Thebans right or wrong when, as a sign of their victory, they built a metal trophy?[121] This fact, that is, the building of a metal trophy as a sign of victory, is certainly self-consistent and has all the force of a proof, this being the custom of that population.

53. About the Assumptive Issue

1. An assumptive issue is one that does not possess in itself any stable fact on which to build a defense but has to derive it from external factors. It consists of four parts: namely, confession, rejection of the crime, retort, and comparison.

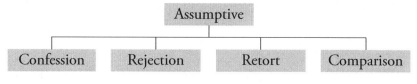

53. The Commentator

1. Tullius defines "assumptive" an issue that is not self-sufficient in the defense from a crime one is charged with but needs external elements to

find the appropriate arguments. For example, when Orestes was accused of his mother's murder, and argued that he had been justified in killing her, the deed appeared so cruel that his statement seemed itself insufficient as a defense but needed an external fact to justify it, which was: "I was justified in murdering her since she had murdered my father."[122] With this addition the argument seemed plausible. 2. Such an assumptive issue consists of four parts, which will be discussed separately.

54. About Confession

1. Confession and admission occur whenever the accused does not defend what he has done, but asks to be forgiven. This issue consists of two parts: exculpation and plea.

54. The Commentator

1. After defining the assumptive issue and the four parts it consists of, Tullius analyzes each of them separately so as to make the juridical situation clearer. 2. First, he defines confession as the issue where the accused admits his crime and confesses that he has committed it but asks to be forgiven. This can occur in two ways: by exculpation or plea. He will deal with both separately, beginning with exculpation.

55. About Exculpation

1. Exculpation occurs whenever the crime is confessed, but the guilt is denied. Three reasons can be alleged for it: ignorance, chance, and necessity.

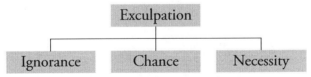

55. The Commentator

1. Tullius explains that the way of admitting a crime called "exculpation" occurs whenever the accused confesses the crime but does not acknowledge his guilt and denies responsibility for the deed. This he can do in three ways, and first of all by claiming ignorance. 2. For example, some Florentine merchants were sailing abroad. There came such a terrible sea storm that they were frightened to the point of offering to give any god that would save them all their goods and of promising to worship him.

In the end, they reached a harbor where Muhammad was worshipped as a god. The merchants worshipped him and gave him rich offerings. They were then accused of having acted against the law, which they surely acknowledged, but protested their ignorance, since they did not know that it was illegal and asked to be acquitted. Therefore, a controversy arose whether they should be punished or not.[123] 3. The second situation implies chance, i.e., an accident which prevents one from doing what he should have done. For instance, a merchant from Cahors had borrowed from a Frenchman a sum of money to be paid in Paris within a certain time and subject to a certain penalty in case of delay. It happened that when the debtor, bringing the money with him, was on his way to Paris, the Rhone was so swollen that it was impossible to sail across it, and therefore it was impossible for him to fulfil his obligations at the indicated time. The other one demanded his penalty, but the merchant replied that he had been unable to deliver the money in time through no fault of his, since an accident had occurred to prevent his coming, and he refused to pay the penalty.[124] The controversy therefore was whether he should pay or not. 4. The third situation concerns necessity, and this occurs whenever it is impossible to act differently from what one did. Here is an example: according to the statutes of Constantinople, all Venetian ships entering the harbor had to be confiscated and given to the emperor. It occurred that two Genoese merchants rented a Venetian ship and loaded it with all sorts of goods, but, because of the strength of the winds and the fury of the storm, against which nothing could be done, they entered the harbor where the ship with all its goods was confiscated by the emperor's men. The merchants admitted that the ship was a Venetian one but claimed to have come to the harbor by sheer necessity and protested that they should not lose their belongings. Therefore, a controversy arose whether they should lose them or not. The Venetians, to whom the ship belonged, demanded either the ship or a sum of money equivalent to its worth, while the merchants maintained that the fine was not due, as they had come to that harbor not of their own will but out of necessity.[125] 5. After dealing with exculpation and its parts, Tullius is now going to deal with the plea.

56. About the Plea

1. The plea occurs when the accused admits that he has committed a crime and that he has acted on purpose, but all the same asks to be forgiven, which is very seldom possible.

56. The Commentator

1. In this brief section of his treatise Tullius shows what is the meaning of "plea" in the art of rhetoric, and says that you have a plea when the accused confesses the crime he is accused of and admits of having committed it on purpose, but nevertheless asks for forgiveness. 2. This can occur in two ways, directly or indirectly. An example of a direct plea is as follows. The accused says: "I admit I have committed this crime, but for the love and the devotion toward God, I ask to be forgiven." The indirect one is: "I confess this crime, and do not ask for your forgiveness, but if you think of how well I have behaved toward the Commune, and how much honor I have brought to it, you might take into consideration to forgive my crime." 3. However, Tullius says that this can seldom occur, especially when there are judges *a lege* who have no power to forgive.[126] Sometimes the emperor or the Senate can forgive serious crimes, as the case was with the Elders in Florence, who had the power to condemn or forgive as they thought fit.[127] 4. After dealing with the first part of the assumptive issue, that is, with confession, and with its two aspects, namely, exculpation and plea, Tullius will discuss the second part, i.e., the rejection of the crime.

57. About the Rejection of the Crime

1. The rejection of the crime occurs whenever the accused tries to avert the crime from himself and charge another man with it, attributing the guilt to the power and action of the latter. This can be done in two ways: by attributing to another person either the guilt or the deed itself. The guilt or the motive are certainly attributed to another person by stating that the crime was committed through his force and power, while the deed is ascribed to another when we maintain that he was likely to commit it or capable of doing so.

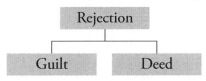

57. The Commentator

1. In this section Tullius defines the rejection of the crime and explains how it can be achieved. For example: one man is accused of a crime and defends himself either by attributing the evil deed to another person or by admitting the crime but maintaining that he was compelled to commit it

by someone who had power and authority over him. The rejection of the crime—Tullius says—can be pleaded in two ways: either by attributing the guilt to another man or by ascribing to him the deed itself. 2. The guilt and the motive are attributed to another when the accused maintains that he committed the deed under the influence of one who had power and authority over him. For example: the Commune of Florence chose some ambassadors who were ordered to obtain money from the bursar for their expenses and to go immediately to the pope and ask him to deny passage on his lands to the knights who were coming from Sicily to Tuscany to attack Florence. The ambassadors asked for the money, but the lord and the bursar refused to give it to them, so they did not go, and the knights came to Tuscany. Of this the ambassadors were therefore accused, but they rejected the charge and accused instead the lord and the bursar who had not given them their dues by availing themselves of their power and authority.[128] 3. If the deed is attributed to another person, this means that the accused denies having committed it and ascribes it to another man, showing that he was likely to do it and capable of doing it. For example: while Cato and Catiline were going from Rome to Rieti, they met a relative of Cato's whom Catiline greatly hated because of the Rome conspiracy, so he killed him outright on the road. Cato had been unable to defend him because he was ill but stayed with the dead man to provide for his burial. Catiline instead, quickly and secretly, went away. The people who happened to go by that road saw the man who had recently died and Cato by him and thought Cato had committed the crime. So he was accused of the murder and defended himself by saying that he had not committed that crime nor could he have done it since the man was a relative of his; moreover, he was ill and unable to do such a thing. Therefore, he transferred the deed and the guilt onto Catiline, since he could do it because the murdered man was his enemy and he himself was strong, healthy, and of an evil disposition.[129] 4. After discussing the rejection of the crime, Tullius is going to define the retort of the charge.

58. Tullius Defines the Retort of a Crime

1. A retort occurs whenever the crime is claimed to have been committed lawfully since the accused had first been offended.

58. The Commentator

1. Tullius explains that the retort of a crime occurs when the accused

claims that he had first been offended, so that the deed was committed lawfully since he had a right to vengeance; this is shown by the example of Orestes, who was accused of the murder of his mother and claimed to have been justified in committing the crime, for she had been the first offender by murdering his own father. Here the question arises whether Orestes was justified in committing that crime or not.[130] 2. After discussing the retort of the crime, Tullius will now define comparison.

59. Tullius Defines Comparison

1. Comparison occurs whenever a deed is argued to be right and useful and the contested crime is claimed to have been committed so as to make the occurrence of the first event possible.

59. The Commentator

1. In this section Tullius explains that comparison occurs whenever the accused claims to have committed the crime he is accused of so that some other event, good and useful, could be made possible. For example: Marcus Tullius, because of the high office he held in Rome, heard that a conspiracy was being planned against the Commune but was unable to learn either who was planning it or how it was being organized. He eventually gave a great sum of money from the city coffers to a woman called Fulvia, the mistress of a man, Quintus Curtius, who knew about the conspiracy; through her he was then able to learn all the details so that he could save the city and the Commune from the high treason that had been perpetrated.[131] 2. However, he was eventually accused of having wasted too much of the city's money. He defended himself by claiming that he had taken the money in order to achieve something useful and right; that is, to prevent the destruction of Rome, a result he could not have obtained in any other way. So he showed that the deed he was accused of had been committed for a good cause. 3. After dealing with the four parts of the assumptive issue, which is a subdivision of the judicial one, as is clear from his treatise on issues, Tullius will briefly focus on those details of the translative issue that have been neglected before.

60. Hermagoras as the Inventor of the Translative Issue

1. The fourth issue, which is called "translative," concerns who should bring the action and against whom, how it should be discussed and before

what court, in what period or under what legislation, and, in any case, it includes all kinds of controversies that tend to change or weaken the action. Hermagoras is commonly believed to have been the inventor of this issue, not because it had not often been used by the ancient rhetoricians but because the theoreticians of this art did not consider it one of the most important and did not include it in their lists of issues. After he found it, however, many criticized it, not out of ignorance, we believe, but to all evidence because of envy and malice.

60. The Commentator

1. This section of Tullius's treatise is very clear and self-evident, especially because the question or issue named "translative" has exhaustively been dealt with in the preceding parts of the book, where many examples are given to show how the action changes when it is not raised either by or against the right person, before the right court, at the right time, and according to the right legislation. In conclusion, the translative issue always aims at either suppressing the action altogether, as is shown by the previous example of the man who says to his adversary "I will not answer your accusation either now or ever," thereby canceling the action, or weakening it in part, though not completely, as is shown in the example of the man who answers his adversary: "I am going to explain my action, but not now," or perhaps, "not before this court."[132] Tullius says that Hermagoras was the inventor of the translative issue, since he included it in the four issues that have been described before. Because of this he was blamed by some people, who were not really wise but envious and slanderous toward him. To be envious is to suffer because of other people's welfare, while to slander is to speak evil of another person.

61. Tullius Promises to Give Examples of Each Issue

1. The issues and their parts have already been dealt with, but examples will be more conveniently found when we have given a great wealth of arguments for each of them, since then the reason for the argument will be clearer whenever the example can fit the kind of case under discussion.

61. The Commentator

1. Tullius illustrates the plan of his book by briefly repeating what he has already defined, i.e., the genera of the issues and their parts, but he will

give examples of each kind, i.e., of the deliberative, the demonstrative, and the judicial, only when the book focuses on each of them. So he proceeds according to the sequence he wishes to give to the teaching of the art of rhetoric.

62. About Simple and Complex Cases

1. Once the issue of a case has been found, it is appropriate to determine whether the case is simple or complex. If it is complex, one should establish whether it is so because it is composed of several questions or because it involves a comparison. Examples are given of each of these, as follows.

62. The Commentator

1. After discussing how to find the issues and their parts, the book explains how to distinguish a simple case, consisting of one fact only, from a complex one, i.e., one made up of two or more facts. In this case, it should be determined whether it is composed of several questions or involves comparison. Examples are given of each of these, as follows.

63. About the Simple Case

1. A simple case is one involving only one clear-cut question, such as: "Are we going to engage in a war against the Corinthians or not?"

63. The Commentator

1. Tullius defines a simple case as one that involves only one fact and one question. For example: the city of Corinth was rebellious against Rome, so the Roman consuls enquired whether an army should be sent against the Corinthians or not. It is easy to see that a simple case consists of a yes-or-no question.

64. About the Complex Case

1. A complex case consists of several questions that are raised on a certain subject. For example: "Is Carthage to be destroyed, handed back to its inhabitants, or rebuilt somewhere else?"

64. The Commentator

1. After discussing the simple case, Tullius proceeds to define the complex

one, which he defines as the case that involves two, three, or four questions. For example: the Romans conquered the city of Carthage, and some claimed that it should be destroyed, others that it should be given back to its inhabitants, and others that it should be rebuilt somewhere else.[133] So, it is evident that the case involves the three questions mentioned above.

65. About the Complex Case Involving Comparison

1. Comparison involves a discussion about the best and the most appropriate course to take in a certain situation. For example: "Should an army be sent to Macedonia against Philip to help the soldiers there, or should it be kept in Italy in order to have the greatest possible military force against Hannibal?"

65. The Commentator

1. After discussing the complex case, where more questions are involved, Tullius focuses on the kind of complex case which involves the comparison between two, three, or four questions, where the best course to be taken must be chosen among two, three, or more alternatives, and it must be decided whether they are all equally good or one is better than the others, in order to find the very best of them. 2. For instance: the Romans had sent an army to Macedonia against Philip, the king of that country, while at the same time they were engaged in a war against Hannibal, who was marching against them with his army. Some senators in Rome claimed that more soldiers should be sent to Macedonia to help those who were fighting there, while others thought that it was wiser to keep the soldiers in Italy to gather an imposing army against Hannibal. The controversy, therefore, was about the better and more appropriate course to take, i.e., whether to keep soldiers in Italy or send them abroad.[134]

66. About Controversies in Written or in Argumentative Form

1. Furthermore, it should be considered whether the controversy is based on written documents or on arguments alone.

66. The Commentator

1. After defining the simple and the complex cases, as well as the ones involving comparison, Tullius proceeds to discuss controversies that arise

from written documents, as well as those deriving from arguments, that is, based on words and questions that are not in written form. In this way, Tullius is going to cover all possible cases and matters by means of rhetoric and will deal with the written cases and the non-written ones separately, as will be apparent from what follows.

67. About Controversies Arising from Written Documents

1. Written controversies arise from some features of written documents. There are five kinds of them, and they are separate from the issues. Sometimes the very words seem inconsistent with the writer's intention, or at times two or more laws appear to contradict one another; occasionally, what is written seems ambiguous; at times something can be inferred from a written document which is not explicitly mentioned there; sometimes the meaning of a word is questioned, as it occurs in the definitional issue. This is why we say that the first kind is of writing and intention, the second of contradictory laws, the third of ambiguity, the fourth of inference, and the fifth of definition.

67. The Commentator

1. After showing what a case about one or more facts consists of, Tullius is going to discuss controversies arising from written documents as distinct from those which have no written text at their origin. He first deals with the written ones, that is, those arising from a written text. These can be of five kinds. 2. The first is called "of writing and intention," since what is written does not appear to correspond to the author's intention. For example, there was a law in the city of Lucca which was written in the following words: "Whoever opens the city gates at night in wartime shall be beheaded." A certain knight opened them to let in some horsemen and soldiers who had come to help the city; so he was condemned to be beheaded according to the written law, but he argued that the interpretation of the law according to the legislator's intention was to punish whoever opened the gate for evil purposes, so the written words did not seem to correspond to the intention of the person who had written them; therefore, a controversy arose whether the actual words or the legislator's intention should be taken into account.[135] 3. The second type involves conflicting laws, whenever two or more of them appear to contradict one another. For instance: according to a law, whoever murdered a tyrant could obtain from the Senate any reward he wished. A tyrant is one who by physical

strength, by means of money, or with the help of armies subjects people to his own power. Another law established that, once the tyrant was dead, five of his closest relatives should be killed. It occurred that a woman murdered her husband who was a tyrant and as a reward asked the Senate that one of her children should be spared. This was possible according to the first law, while the second established that he should die. These were evidently two conflicting laws, and the question arose whether her son should be spared or killed.[136] 4. The third kind is called "ambiguous," since what is written appears to have two or more possible interpretations. For example, Alexander wrote in his will: "I direct that, after my death, my heir should give Cassandro a hundred golden bowls, which he can choose as best he likes." After Alexander's death, Cassandro went to the heir and asked for the hundred golden bowls he liked best. But the heir said: "I must give you the ones I like."[137] So, in the sentence "the ones he can choose as best he likes" Alexander's intention is ambiguous and a controversy arises between the two. 5. The fourth type is called "inferential," since something that is not in the written document can be deduced from it. For instance: Marcellus went into the Church of Saint Peter in Rome, broke the crucifix, and cut all the images from it. He was accused, but no law against such an evil crime could be found; on the other hand, it was impossible for him to get away without some kind of punishment. The accuser therefore tried to derive an appropriate punishment from the existing laws.[138] 6. The fifth kind concerns definition, since the meaning and the force of the written word appear to be questioned, so that it is appropriate that it should be well defined and the possible interpretation clearly indicated. For example: one law states that if the captain of a ship abandons it when there is a storm, and another one manages to rescue it, the ship becomes his. It occurred that a ship was sailing from Pisa to Tunis when a terrible storm broke out near the harbor, so the captain left the ship in a small boat; one man, who was ill, did not leave the ship until the sea was calm again and the ship was able to dock. Therefore, he claimed that the ship was his by force of law, since the captain had abandoned it when he had jumped into the small boat, while he himself had rescued it. The captain answered that by getting into the small boat he had not abandoned the ship, so that a controversy arose about the meaning of "abandon";[139] this shows that, in order to understand the full meaning of a word, this should be defined, and the writer's intention clearly stated. 7. After discussing the controversy based on written documents as well as its five types, Tullius will now focus on the controversy based on argument alone.

68. About the Controversy Arising from Argumentation

1. This kind of controversy occurs whenever there is no written document, and the whole question is based on argumentation.

68. The Commentator

1. A controversy based on argumentation occurs whenever there is no written document to take into consideration, but the proof is only obtained by means of logical reasoning, independently of any written text. For example: Anibaldo claims that Italy is a better country than France, while Lodoigo denies that, so that a controversy arises between them.[140] Therefore, each one has to find suitable arguments to prove what he says, for there is neither anything written on the subject, nor is it a matter of law.

69. About the Four Parts of the Case

1. After the nature of the case has been considered and the issue explained, after the simple and the complex cases have been defined, and a distinction has been made between those who are based on written documents and those based on reasoning alone, now the question, the reason, the judgment, and the defender's justification, which all derive from the issue, must be analyzed.

69. The Commentator

1. In this section, after mentioning the possible kinds of cases, namely, the deliberative, the demonstrative, and the judicial; after defining the issue, and its various types, i.e., conjectural, definitional, translative, and legal; after distinguishing between the simple and the complex issue, that is, the ones involving one or more questions; and defining those based on written documents as distinct from those involving only logical reasoning—all matters that have been exhaustively dealt with by the Commentator—Tullius begins to discuss extensively the question, the reason, the judgment, and the defendant's argument of the case, all of which arise from the issue, which can be said to be at the basis of these proceedings.

70. About the Question

1. A question is a controversy arising from a conflict concerning the motives of an action, such as: "You were not justified in doing that"/"I was

justified." This is the conflict about the causes of a deed that establishes the issue and wherefrom the controversy, which is called a "question," arises about whether something was justified or not.

70. The Commentator

1. In the preceding section Tullius explains what a question is and defines it as the subject of the debate from which a controversy arises, where one accuses and the other defends a certain action. For example, the accuser says: "You were not justified in taking my horse," while the defender retorts: "Yes, I was." Now the case is set, that is, everyone has clearly spoken, one accusing and the other defending what has been done. This is called the "issue." 2. On this rests the decision whether the action was justified or not. This is what Tullius calls a "question." Therefore, we can conclude that, when the parts have spoken, i.e., the accuser has brought the charge, and the defender has rejected it, the case can be said to have been established and set, and is now called the "issue"; thus, it must be determined whether the defense is right or wrong; i.e., when one says, "I was justified in doing it," one must prove it, and this is what Tullius calls a "question." 3. Therefore, the plea of the accused, "I was justified," is worth nothing unless the reason is given, and this is what now Tullius is going to define.

71. About the Reason of a Case

1. The reason is what upholds the case. If it did not exist, there would be no controversy. This will be shown, by way of example, by the following episode, simple and clear. If Orestes, once he was charged with the murder of his mother, had not claimed: "I was justified in doing it, since she had murdered my father," he would have had no defense, without which no controversy would have arisen. So the reason for this case is that his mother had murdered Agamemnon.

71. The Commentator

1. As it appears from Tullius's text, the reason is what holds the case together so that, if the accused does not give the reason for his action, no controversy can arise, and he cannot have any defense; therefore, the accusation still holds and there is no debate. 2. For example: it is true that Orestes's mother murdered her husband, i.e., Orestes's father. For this reason, Orestes, overcome with grief, murdered her. He was accused of the crime

and confessed it but claimed that he had been justified in doing it.[141] But unless he had given the motive of his action, his defense would have been worth nothing, and neither controversy nor question would have arisen. 3. But since he said "I was justified in doing it, for she had murdered my father," there was a defense and the case was valid, the reason and motives of the murder having been clearly explained. After showing what a reason and a question are, Tullius will discuss the judgment.

72. About the Judgment

1. The point for the judgment is a kind of controversy that arises from either weakening or confirming the reason of an action. Let us consider the justifying reason in the example that has just been given: "She had murdered my father." The wise man says: "She should have been killed without your direct intervention; her crime could well have been punished without your cruel participation in it." From the statement of the reason, an important debate arises whether Orestes was justified in murdering his mother because she had killed his father.

72. The Commentator

1. After discussing what the reason of an act is and the way the judgment arises from it, Tullius proceeds to define it, i.e., to explain how, where, and when it can be delivered. For example: the accused gives a reason for his action and bases his defense on it. The accuser argues against such defense and weakens the reason of the accused. From the strengthening of the defense on the one side and the weakening of it on the other, a question called the "point for the judgment" arises since, once the case is clear, it is possible to decide about it. 2. Let us consider once more the example given above. Orestes gives as the reason for having killed his mother Clytemnestra the fact that she had murdered his father Agamemnon, thus strengthening his defense. But his accuser argues: "You should not have murdered your mother for it, but others could have done that without the ruthless and cruel action of a son who murders his own mother." In this way, Orestes's reason was weakened, and he was exposed to scorn and abomination. From the strengthening of his motives on the one side and the weakening of them on the other, the question called the "judgment" arises, since now a decision has become possible. 3. So, after defining the question, the reason, and the judgment, Tullius will discuss justification.

73. About the Justification

1. Justification is the closest and strongest argument offered to judgment, as if, for instance, Orestes explained that the same attitude his mother had toward his own father, she had toward himself, his sisters, the kingdom, his noble descent, and his renowned family, so that her children were justified in taking the matter in their own hands and punishing her themselves.

73. The Commentator

1. After defining the question, the reason of an action, and the judgment, the justification is now discussed. Tullius's teaching has certainly a logical sequence: first, the question concerns a controversy between people where one is accused of having committed a crime without being justified in doing it, while the accused defends himself by claiming either that he has done well or that he was right in doing what he did. So the question arises whether he was right or wrong. Then the accused explains why he acted as he did, and this is called his "reason." After the accused has given his reason, his opponent argues against it and weakens the strongest point in the argument of the accused, and this is called the "judgment."

73. The Justification

1. Once the judgment has been given, the accused should find all his arguments against it as firmly as he can. For example: Orestes says that he murdered his mother since she had killed his father, and this is the reason he gives for his crime; his opponent, in judging his action, claims that he should not have done that himself but let other people do it, and in this way he weakens the other's reasons. Now Orestes must produce very sound arguments, such as: "Just as she had killed my father, she had planned to murder me and my sisters to whom she had herself given birth, to destroy our kingdom, to soil our good name, and to endanger our family."[142] By these arguments, he strongly defends his motives against the object of the verdict when he says: "Since she had behaved in such an evil way and had planned such great cruelty, it was after all appropriate that her own children, and no one else, should punish her." These are strong arguments because his mother's behavior is said to have been cruel, proud, and malicious. A deed is proud when it is committed against one's superiors, as Clytemnestra did when she killed King Agamemnon;[143] it is cruel when it is directed against one's own relatives, as she did by acting against her own family; it is malicious when it is really unbelievable, since it is against nature for a woman to murder her

husband and children and to destroy a noble kingdom. Such very sound arguments that the accused opposes to emphasize his motives and against the weakening of them on the part of the accuser are called a "justification."

74. Issues Where No Judgment Is Required

1. Similar judgments can be found in other issues. In the conjectural issue, however, since no reason can be given in it (the fact not being admitted), no judgment involving a debate about the reasons of an action can exist; therefore, the question and object of the verdict coincide: "it was done"; "it was not"; "was it, or was it not done?" As a matter of fact, one can find as many questions, reasons, judgments, and justifications as there are issues or parts of them in a case

74. The Commentator

1. In this section Tullius explains that, as has been said before, judgments can be found in every issue, except in the conjectural one, which has been extensively discussed above, because no judgment can be given of what the accused does not justify but denies having committed. 2. For instance, Ulysses was accused of having murdered Ajax, but he said: "I did not do it," thereby rejecting the accusation.[144] Therefore, he cannot give any reasons for a deed he denies having committed, and his opponent has no way to weaken the reasons of the accused. In this case, no judgment can exist. Therefore, in a conjectural issue question and judgment coincide: where the accuser says "You murdered him" and Ulysses answers, "I did not," the question and the judgment are whether he murdered him or not. 3. Tullius further states that there are as many reasons, judgments, and justifications as there are issues in a case.

75. About the Other Parts of the Case

1. Once all the elements of a case have been identified, the individual parts must be taken into consideration. As a matter of fact, what must be said first must not necessarily be thought out first, because if you want the opening words of your oration to be closely related to the case, then you must derive from them what you have to say afterward.

75. The Commentator

1. Tullius claims that if the good rhetorician has a good knowledge of his

case and has by now understood all he has been teaching him in this book, when he has to discuss it, he should think carefully and have clearly present to his mind all the parts of his case together, and not separately, before he ever begins to speak. For if he thinks first of what he has to discuss without bearing in mind what he has to say afterward, the beginning of the oration will not be consistent with the middle part or the middle part with the end. 2. On the other hand, whoever chooses his words in agreement with the nature of the case and thinks of what is appropriate to say first and what must be said later will make his beginning perfectly consistent with both the middle part of his oration and the conclusion. This is what a good weaver does, who never thinks first of the wool only but has before his eyes the whole fabric before he begins to work, that is, the wool, the color, the dimensions of the cloth, and provides himself with all the necessary tools his craft requires; only at that point does he begin to weave.[145]

76. About the Six Parts of the Oration

1. When the judgments and those arguments which are necessary to it have carefully been found, accurately and thoughtfully dealt with according to the rules of the art of rhetoric, the other parts of the oration must be arranged, and in our opinion there are six of them: exordium, narration, partition, confirmation, refutation, and conclusion.

76. The Commentator

1. After he has exhaustively discussed the well-planned case and has recommended to the good rhetorician to think out all the parts of his case in order to relate the middle part and the conclusion of his oration with the exordium, so that words appear to come naturally one from the other, Tullius says that, after all this has been done, the point for the judgment of the case has been established with all that is needed according to the rules of rhetoric (which should be followed with the greatest attention and decision), the other parts of the oration that have not yet been discussed, the six of them, must carefully be analyzed; and this is what the book is going to do.

76. The Commentator Explains What Has Been Said Before

2. Now, before the exposition proceeds, the Commentator wishes to ask his host,[146] for the love of whom this treatise has been written, not without

great anxiety, to pay the greatest attention to what has been said and will be said in what follows, in order to learn it and store it in his memory, whether he wishes to become an accomplished letter writer or a noble rhetorician, this book being a source and guiding light for the art. 3. Since the book deals with controversies, explains how to speak in matters that are the objects of debates, discusses cases and questions, and frequently mentions, by way of example, the accuser and the accused, a superficial reader might believe that Tullius deals with trials that take place in law courts and with nothing else. 4. But the Commentator is perfectly aware that his friend has such great discretion that he sees and grasps the real aim of the book and, further, that he knows that trials are best dealt with by jurists, while rhetoric shows how to speak appropriately on a certain case which is not necessarily to be tried in court, nor always to occur between an accuser and an accused, but concerns other matters as well, such as the correct language in diplomatic missions, in councils of lords and of Communes, as well as the style of a well-composed letter.[147] 5. Since Tullius claims that issues, questions, reasons, judgments, and justifications exist if there is a debate, an intelligent person should understand that when people discuss different matters, it often occurs that everyone gives his opinion in his own way and the other argues in the opposite way, so that a conflict arises; one claims, the other defends; the first is called the "accuser," the opponent is named the "defender," and the object of the debate is called the "case." 6. But if one accuses and the other denies having committed what he is accused of, there can be no question except to ascertain whether the fact has actually been committed by him or not. When, however, one accuses and the other defends, this means that a case has started and has been established between them. This is the issue which is at the basis of the question, i.e., whether the arguments of the defense are right or wrong; moreover, everyone debates as he likes best to support his own words and weaken his adversary's, as is clear from what has been said before about the question, the reason, the judgment, and the justification. 7. Therefore, as the examples given above clearly show, nobody should believe that Orestes was tried in court for the murder of his mother, but that there was a debate among people, where some claimed that he had not been justified in committing the murder, and these were the accusers, while some defended Orestes and claimed he had been justified in murdering her. In this book Orestes is called the "accused."

76. About Counselors

8. The same occurs with the counselors of lords or of Communes when they meet to advise on some matter, that is, on some case that has been proposed to them, and they have different opinions about it, so that the issue of the case is established; a debate among them begins, whereby a question arises whether one has advised well or not. This is what Tullius calls a "question." 9. Therefore, as soon as one has said or advised what he thinks is appropriate, he immediately gives the reason why he believes his advice good and correct; this is what Tullius calls the "reason." 10. After he has done that, he endeavors to show why, if anybody advised to the contrary, this would be both evil and wrong, thus weakening the part that opposes his advice. This is what Tullius calls the "judgment." 11. After he has weakened his opponents, he tries to collect the closest possible arguments and the strongest reasons he can find in order to weaken the opponent further and give greater force to his own reasons. This is what Tullius calls the "justification." 12. The above-mentioned four parts, i.e., question, reason, judgment, and justification, can all be included in the oration of one of the speakers, as it appears from what has been said before. He can, however, limit his speech to the question, only expressing his opinion without giving any other reasons. The oration can also involve two parts, when the opinion and the reason are given, or perhaps three, if the opinion and the reason are given, but the opponent's argument is also weakened. Finally, it can involve all four parts, as has been shown before. 13. This is the first orator's speech. When he has given his advice and has concluded his oration, another counselor stands up and says exactly the opposite of what has hitherto been claimed: so the issue is established, the case started, and the debate begins; and from the various opinions expressed in the orations, the question arises whether the first counselor has advised well or not. The opponent then shows the reason why his advice is better than the other's. Further on, he weakens what the first speaker has said or advised, after which he confirms his own opinion with all the arguments he can find. Therefore, the above-mentioned four parts can be found in the first orator's speech, in the second speaker's oration, and in the words of all the other speakers. 14. In the same way, it often happens that two people exchange letters in Latin, in prose, in verse, or in the vernacular, Tuscan or other, where they argue about a certain subject, and a controversy arises. A lover, in pleading mercy of his woman, gives his own reasons in many words, while the woman defends and strengthens her point of view by opposing and weakening the pleader's arguments. This example and many

others clearly show that Tullius's teaching of rhetoric is not limited to contending in law courts, although no one can be a good advocate, let alone a perfect one, unless he speaks according to the art of rhetoric.

15. It is true that the above discussion seems to concern mainly those facts that involve controversy and debate between people who are opposed to each other; it could be argued that letters do not always involve contention (when, for instance, one, being in love, composes songs and verses to his lady, where no controversy at all exists between him and the woman). Therefore, Tullius and the Commentator might be blamed for not giving instruction about what are by far the most frequent situations, especially the writing of letters, which involve a much greater number of people than the activity of the orator or of the public speaker. 16. But if the natures of a letter or of a song are carefully considered, it is easy to see that whoever composes a poem or sends a letter wishes to obtain something from the addressee, and this can be done by pleading, asking, ordering, threatening, comforting, or advising, and the same applies to the receiver of the letter, who can defend himself or refuse what he is asked by the same means. But whoever sends a letter uses ornate and wise words together with sound arguments in order to persuade the other not to refuse what he asks and to weaken or demolish any pretext or excuse the other might advance. Therefore, there is a silent contention between them, and almost all letters or love songs involve a conflict, either silent or explicit. If it were not so—Tullius clearly states when explaining the aim of the book—they would have nothing to do with rhetoric. 17. Therefore, whether it is a matter of conflict or not, Tullius endeavors above all to teach how to speak or write letters according to the rules of rhetoric. In any case, whenever Tullius appeared to be too hasty in his exposition, or perhaps to be concerned only with the teaching of contention, the Commentator endeavored, with his modest abilities, to supply information, clearly and exhaustively, so that his friend could understand both subjects.[148] 18. Here Tullius begins to discuss those parts of an oration or of a dictated letter he has not mentioned before. There are six of them, as it appears from the diagram-tree below.

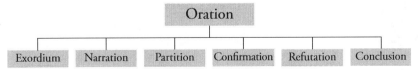

These are the six parts Tullius believes to be always present in orations and letters, especially when they involve controversies, as the Commentator has shown above, and, as can be found in another part of this book, Tullius traces all rhetoric back to cases which involve controversy and debate and maintains that those words that are not spoken in a conflict, where one is opposed to another person, do not belong to the form and the art of rhetoric. 19. But a dictated letter is often not concerned with controversy or debate but is rather a present one sends to another person. In it it is the mind that speaks, and somebody who is silent can be heard to ask and plead from a distant land, thus obtaining good will, which causes love to be enforced and to thrive, considering that many things can be expressed in writing which one would not have the courage or the ability to say in his addressee's presence. The Commentator will therefore briefly discuss some wise people's opinion and state his own about that part of rhetoric which concerns letter writing, as he promised at the beginning of this treatise. 20. He defines it as a correct and ornate way of dealing with any thing in a manner that is suitable to the subject matter;[149] it is therefore appropriate to understand every word of this definition of letter writing. "Correct" refers to the right construction of the words used in a letter, where subject and verb, masculine and feminine, singular and plural, first, second, and third person, that is, all the parts of grammar, must be in the right relationship, as the Commentator will explain further on, these rules applying both to rhetoric and to letter writing. 21. "Ornate" means that the whole letter should be composed of pleasant and appropriate words, full of good counsel, and this is also required of all parts of rhetoric, as has been said before in the commentary to Tullius's text. 22. "Dealing with any thing" indicates, as Boethius says,[150] that anything one proposes to say can be the subject of the letter writer, and this is different from Tullius's statement, according to which the orator's subject is limited to three aspects only, namely, the demonstrative, the deliberative, and the judicial. He says "in a manner that is suitable to the subject matter" because the words the dictator uses must fit the subject of the letter, for he could easily use well-constructed and ornate words, but this would be worth nothing unless they suited the subject. 23. So the definition of the letter writer is different with respect to what Tullius says. From the teaching of these two different skills, that is, eloquence and letter writing, the Commentator's friend will be able to choose the right course. Because of these differences, it is convenient to distinguish the parts of the letter from those of the oration, of which, as Tullius explains, there are six: namely, exordium, narration, partition, confirmation, refutation, and conclusion. 24. (1) According to Tullius, the exordium is the first part of the oration; it prepares the mind of the audience to what follows, and is commonly called "the prologue"; (2) the narration is that part of the oration where things that have actually occurred are described and things that have not occurred are told as if they had really happened. This is found whenever the fact, which is to become the subject of the oration, is mentioned. (3) Partition occurs whenever the orator, having told an episode, makes a clear distinction between his opinion and that of his opponent by saying: "this was so, and that in this other way"; he then accepts those reasons that are more favorable to him and most harmful to his opponent and persuades the audience that he has told the whole fact. (4) Confirmation is defined as that part of the oration where the orator offers arguments and gives reasons to add authority and truthfulness to his case. (5) Refutation occurs whenever the opponent's opinion is weakened and belittled by means of reasons and arguments. (6) Conclusion is the end of the whole oration. 25. These are the six parts that Tullius believes should be in every oration and which will exhaustively be discussed in this book. From what has been said, it is easy to understand that these can also be the parts of a letter, whatever its subject. Three parts—namely, exordium, narration, and conclusion—are equally suitable to an oration and to a letter; the other three—namely, partition, confirmation, and refutation—are either less important in a letter or altogether absent. On the other hand, a letter is composed of five parts, one of which, i.e., salutation, can well be absent in the oration; the other one, petition, though Tullius does not mention it as part of the oration, is such an important part of it that an oration can hardly exist without it. A letter has therefore five parts; namely, salutation, exordium, narration, petition, and conclusion, as it appears from the following diagram:

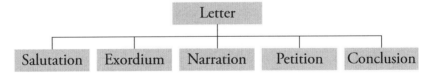

26. Should anyone ask why Tullius neither mentioned salutation nor discussed it in his book, he will find the reason in what follows: in his treatise, Tullius focuses on the orations that are delivered before audiences, where it is unnecessary to mention either the orator's, the opponent's, or the judge's names; on the contrary, the addresser's and the addressee's names are essential in a letter, if their identities must not remain unknown. Moreover, the salutation appears to be part of the exordium, which, in a letter, can be said

to begin with the greetings. Tullius does not mention salutation as part of a letter, although he discusses exordium extensively, since he appears to have given all his attention to defining the kind of rhetoric that concerns controversies and debates. 27. Thus, some scholars claimed that the salutation was not part of the letter but some sort of heading not included in it.[151] I claim, however, that the salutation is the gate, as it were, of the letter, in that it gives people's names and qualifications clearly and in the right order, as well as expressing the addresser's feelings. "Gate" alludes to the entrance into the letter, which specifies the sender's and the receiver's names. "Qualifications" alludes to the rank and position of people, such as "Innocent, Pope"; "Frederick, Emperor"; "Achilles, Knight"; "Oddofredi, Judge";[152] the same applying to the other positions. "The right order" means that names and ranks are mentioned appropriately, while the "sender's feelings" concern words and expressions of good, or perhaps ill, will, according to his disposition. 28. It is therefore evident that the salutation is as part of a letter as the eye is part of a man's body, and just as the eye is a noble part of man's body, so is the salutation a noble part of the letter, since it gives light to it, as the eye lights up a man's face. In fact, a letter without a salutation is like a house without a front door or, perhaps, like a live body without eyes.[153] Therefore, whoever says that the salutation is a heading external to the letter is wrong; on the contrary, it is firmly included and sealed in it, while the heading of the letter is the address which indicates to whom the letter must be sent. 29. There are, however, cases when no salutation is present, either because the sender wishes to keep the addressee's name secret, in case the letter should fall into alien hands, or for other reasons.[154] Moreover, I am not saying that greetings should be included in all letters. Sometimes, love, pleasure, or amusement suggest that other words expressing greater intimacy or playfulness, instead of mere greetings, can be used. Greetings should not be sent to one's superiors and should be replaced by expressions of reverence or devotion. Sometimes, we omit salutations when we write to our enemies and only mention their names, or perhaps write other words expressing indignation, encouragement to do well, or something of the kind. So does the pope when writing to the Jews or to other people who are not of our Catholic religion or to the enemies of the Holy Church: he omits salutation and occasionally replaces it by expressions such as: "be better advised," "get to know the way to truth," "be engaged in works of charity," or some sentences to the same effect.[155]

30. Therefore, the good letter writer, just as he does when he meets somebody in person, should endeavor to put salutation in a letter by using

such ornate words as the rank of the addressee requires. For when one is admitted to the presence of the pope, the emperor, or any other religious or lay authority, he reverently bows his head and at times even kneels before them to kiss the pope's or the emperor's foot; in exactly the same way, the letter writer must mention the name of the receiver and his position with the due reverence, and place it at the beginning of his letter; he should then indicate his own name and position, and then mention what he wishes to tell the addressee as far as greetings or any other expressions that might be convenient are concerned, but taking care to show his feelings in an appropriate manner and in words suitable both to the addresser and the addressee. 31. For when we write to people who are our superior, inferior, or equal, we must endeavor to use expressions suitable to their ranks and positions. Though I said that the name of the superior or of the person of equal rank should be put at the top of the letter, I have seen great princes and lords put the receiver's name at the top when writing to lesser people or to merchants; this is against the rules of the art, but they do it for practical purposes, to obtain some advantage. Let therefore the letter writer be careful in every detail, and make an appropriate and convenient salutation, in order to obtain the receiver's favor and benevolence, as we will show following Tullius's rhetoric. 32. This is really a subject the Commentator could discuss at length, and not without great usefulness. However, considering that some niceties, such as the omission of the verb in salutations, the practice of putting the sender's name in the third person out of modesty, and the fact that at times only the first letter of the name is indicated, pertain more to letters written in Latin than to those in the vernacular, the Commentator will omit this discussion and follow Tullius in the definition of the other parts of the oration, and of the letter, according to the plan of his book. Here we stop discussing salutation, and focus on the exordium, which will be dealt with in two ways: one which follows Tullius and appears to concern the oration; and the other which is suitable to both the letter and the oration in addition to what Tullius says in his treatise.

77. Exordium

1. Since the exordium is necessarily the first of all parts, we shall discuss it first.

77. The Commentator

1. Since Tullius wishes to deal with the exordium before the other parts of the oration, he calls it the "prince of them all," and he is certainly right in

this: first, because it is actually pronounced before the other parts; second, because by the exordium we appear to prepare and make the audience's mind ready to understand what we wish to say afterward.

78. About the Exordium

1. The exordium is a statement that prepares in a convenient way the minds of the audience for the words to come, which becomes possible provided the audience are rendered well-disposed, attentive, and compliant. Therefore, to begin one's case well, one should diligently become acquainted with its nature in advance.

78. The Commentator

1. After mentioning the parts of the oration, Tullius discusses each of them separately and first focuses on the exordium, which he deals with in the following way. He begins by defining it and explains that there are three things an orator must do: first, render the audience well-disposed, attentive, and compliant toward what he has to say; this means that he should be perfectly acquainted with the nature of the case he is going to speak or write about. 2. In the second place, he divides the exordium into two parts: the opening and the *insinuatio* and shows in what situations each of them is to be used. 3. In the third place, he shows where we can find the right arguments to obtain benevolence, attention, and compliance, and how these can be used in the parts of the exordium called the "opening" and the *insinuatio*, respectively. 4. In the fourth place, he analyzes the virtues and the faults of the exordium. 5. He therefore defines it as an adornment of words which the orator or the letter writer places at the beginning of his speech by way of prologue, and through which he tries to obtain the audience's attention and compliance, so that they can understand what he says and grasp the force of his words. 6. And if the audience are willing to understand and become acquainted with the nature of the case and the force of the words, they are also attentive; while if they are attentive, it does not follow that they should also be well disposed to understand. These three aspects will be dealt with in due course. 7. However, since the orator who does not know the nature and the kind of the case in advance cannot easily achieve the three aims I have mentioned, that is, the benevolence, the attention, and the good disposition of his audience, in what follows the features of the various cases will be discussed.

79. Kinds of Cases

1. There are five kinds of cases: honorable, inconceivable, insignificant, dubious, and obscure.

79. The Commentator

1. In this short section of his work, Tullius mentions the various kinds of cases; that is, he explains how many types of them exist. Should anyone object that Tullius had first mentioned three kinds of cases only—namely, the deliberative, the demonstrative, and the judicial—while he now says that there are five of them—that is, the honorable, the inconceivable, the insignificant, the dubious, and the obscure—I answer that the first three are substantial qualities, essential parts of the case, and cannot be changed in any way. So, a deliberative case cannot be but deliberative, a demonstrative one cannot be but demonstrative, and the same applies to the judicial case. 2. But an honorable case can well be dishonorable, an inconceivable one can well be conceivable, and the same can be said of the insignificant, the dubious, and the obscure. These are all accidental qualities that can be present or not, while the others are substantial features and cannot be altered.[156]

80. About the Honorable Case

1. A case is honorable if it is immediately agreeable to the mind of the audience, even with no exordium of ours.

80. The Commentator

1. A case can be called "honorable" whenever the orator, without any prologue, can win the mind of those who listen to him, so that they believe and enjoy what the speaker says on the subject of the case. No special words are needed to obtain the benevolence of the audience, because the case is just and honorable in itself, as it happens when someone accuses a burglar, defends one's own father, an orphan, a widow, or a church.

81. About the Inconceivable Case

1. An "inconceivable case" is one toward which there is a negative attitude in the audience's mind.

81. The Commentator

1. An inconceivable case is one the audience cannot like, since it implies something foul and cruel. Therefore, their minds are against us, and their sympathies are alienated; we must then try to get their benevolence back, as it happens in a case where someone is a thief, has set fire to a place, or has murdered his own father. 2. Thus, It is evident that a case can be both honorable and inconceivable, since one can at the same time defend one's own father—thus behaving honorably—and act against one's own mother. From this example all the situations similar to it can easily be understood.

82. About the Insignificant Case

1. An "insignificant case" is one the audience do not take seriously and do not make any effort to understand.

82. The Commentator

1. An insignificant case is one of small importance, so that the audience does not think it is worthy of a great effort to understand it, such as a case concerning a hen or something of equally negligible value. For this case we should endeavor to catch the audience's attention.

83. About the Dubious Case

1. A "dubious case" is one where either the point for the decision is ambiguous or the case itself is partly honorable and partly foul and dishonorable, so that it invites benevolence and hostility at the same time.

83. The Commentator

1. A dubious case is one where there is no certainty about the decision to make and about the chance of arriving at a just verdict, as in the case of Orestes, who claimed to have been justified in murdering his mother both because she had murdered his father and because Apollo had ordered him to do so.[157] So the audience are not certain which of the two reasons must be decided on. 2. Another ambiguous case is one that is in part honorable, so that the audience tend to be favorable to it, and in part dishonorable, and as such the audience do not like it, as in the case *de filio*, where a burglar was accused of a theft, and his son was trying hard to defend him; it was certainly honorable to defend one's own father but dishonorable to defend a thief.[158]

84. About the Obscure Case

1. An "obscure case" is one where either the audience are slow to understand or the case is entangled with many aspects that are difficult to grasp.

84. The Commentator

1. Tullius says that a case is called obscure either when the audience are slow to understand it, that is, they do not catch the implications of the orator's words with the necessary promptness or accuracy because either they are not learned enough or are perhaps tired with what the other orators have said before, or even the case happens to be intricate in itself and includes aspects that are obscure and difficult to grasp.

85. About the Parts of the Exordium

1. Since there are many kinds of cases, all different from one another, it is convenient to plan the exordium in such a way as to suit the nature of each one. The exordium is thus made of two parts, the opening and the *insinuatio*.

85. The Commentator

1. Tullius says that, since there are many different cases, namely, the five kinds he has mentioned above, each different from the others, the exordium should fit the nature of the case about which one has to speak or write letters. 2. Because Tullius wishes to deal with this point clearly, he claims the exordium to be twofold; one of the parts is called the "opening," while the other is the *insinuatio*, and he will discuss both of them exhaustively. We must therefore be conscious that there are five cases an orator or a letter writer may have to deal with: namely, the honorable, the inconceivable, the insignificant, the dubious, and the obscure. To discuss all these kinds of cases, there are only two kinds of exordia, the opening, and the *insinuatio*.

86. About the Opening

1. The "opening" is a speech which directly and briefly wins the audience's benevolence, compliance, or attention.

86. The Commentator

1. The kind of exordium called the "opening" occurs whenever orators and

letter writers at the very start of their speeches, without many words and arti-
fice, but speaking clearly and openly, make the audience's mind benevolent
and well disposed toward themselves and their cases, and sometimes even
compliant and attentive; this Pompey did when, speaking to the Romans
about the necessity of the war against Julius Caesar, began his oration in the
following way: "Since we have Right on our side and fight to defend our right-
fulness and our Commune, we must be hopeful that the gods will help us."[159]

87. About *Insinuatio*

1. *Insinuatio* is a way of speaking which indirectly and covertly reaches the
minds of the audience.

87. The Commentator

1. Tullius calls *insinuatio* that kind of the exordium where orators or letter
writers make a long prologue of dissembling words, pretending to yearn
after what they do not really care about and to despise what they actually
yearn after, so they beat about the bush with many words in order to dis-
concert the audience's minds and make them benevolent, compliant, and
attentive, as it occurred when Sinon said to those who caused him to be in
grievous distress: "Till now, I have asked you to relieve me of such pains;
now I only ask for death, but I would have given a huge treasure to anyone
who had saved me." In this way he surreptitiously pretended not to long
for what he actually desired in order to suggest that he should be saved for
money, since he was unworthy of their pity.[160] 2. Now that the opening
and the *insinuatio* have been clearly explained, in what follows Tullius will
show which of these two aspects of the exordium should be used in each of
the five kinds of cases, i.e., in the honorable, the insignificant, the inconceivable, the dubious, and the obscure.

88. About the Inconceivable Case

1. In the inconceivable case, if the audience are not too unsympathetic, we
could win their benevolence by means of what has been called the "opening." But if they are too ill disposed toward us, then we should turn to the
insinuatio, since, if one wanted to obtain so cheaply sympathy and benevolence from people who are enraged, one would only succeed in increasing
and kindling the others' hatred.

88. The Commentator

1. The inconceivable case has previously been clearly defined as one consisting of the defense of something foul, and is therefore one toward which the audience is not well disposed. However, Tullius argues that occasionally, when an inconceivable case is presented, the audience may happen not to be too angry with us. In this case we can obtain their benevolence by means of that kind of exordium which is called the "opening," that is, by means of a prologue of few and clear words. 2. But if the audience are really angry and ill disposed toward us, it is certainly much more appropriate to turn to the second kind, namely, the *insinuatio*, and start with a prologue of insincere and ambiguous words, so that we can soften their souls and win back their benevolence and sympathy. As a matter of fact, when the audience is angry and unsympathetic, if one wanted to win it back by speaking at once briefly and openly, one would probably increase its anger and kindle its hatred; this is why one has to face the question softly and in a not-too-direct way.

89. About the Insignificant Case

1. When the case is insignificant, one should endeavor to obtain the audience's attention in order to remove their anger and scorn.

89. The Commentator

1. When the case is insignificant, that is, of negligible importance, so that the audience do not make great efforts to understand it, the kind of exordium called the "opening" should be used in such a way as to win the audience's attention. This can easily be done by making the case appear more important and lofty than it actually is, as Virgil did when he decided to speak about bees: "I will say great and wonderful things about the small bees."[161]

90. About the Dubious Case

1. In the dubious case, if the reason of an act is doubtful, the *exordium* should begin from this one. But if the case is in part honorable and in part dishonorable, it would be more appropriate to try and obtain benevolence by dealing with it as if the whole case could be considered honorable.

90. The Commentator

1. The dubious case has already been said before to be of two kinds: in one of them, the reason is doubtful, as it appears in the example concerning Orestes, who claimed that there had been two reasons that justified the murder of his mother. In this case he had to begin his *exordium* from the very reason he most wanted to emphasize and which he believed to be most useful to him. 2. But if the case is dubious, because it is partly honorable and partly dishonorable, then the good orator must win the benevolence of the audience by means of the kind of exordium called the "opening" so that the whole case may seem honorable.

91. About the Honorable Case

1. When the case is an honorable one, we can either omit the opening and, if we believe that it is more appropriate, begin our oration from its legal aspects or from some very sound argument. But if we wish to start with the opening, we should use all the arguments capable of increasing the benevolence the case has already won.

91. The Commentator

1. When the case we have to discuss is an honorable one, we have naturally the audience's benevolence and do not need to adorn our oration with many words. Therefore, we can easily omit the opening as well as the exordium and the prologue, and begin by stating the facts of the case, quoting the laws that are appropriate to it, or presenting the strongest and most certain argument we can find. 2. However, if one wishes to begin with an opening or a prologue, this should be done not to obtain benevolence but to increase it. Therefore, in this case, our opening should consist of words appropriate to the benevolence the case deserves.

92. About the Obscure Case

1. In an obscure case, we should make the audience compliant by an appropriate opening.

92. The Commentator

1. The obscure case has already been defined. Tullius claims that for the case we call "obscure", we should use that part of the exordium called

the "opening" in such a way as to make the audience compliant, that is, by briefly stating the main features of the fact from both sides, to make them understand and grasp the nature of the case. Then, when we see that the audience are ready to understand it, we can proceed with our arguments, as the case requires.

93. About the Ways of Obtaining Benevolence

1. Once we have discussed what can be done by means of the exordium, we turn to the methods by which these results can be obtained.

93. The Commentator

1. Hitherto Tullius has shown what the exordium should be like and what kind of *exordium* should be used in each case in order to win the audience's benevolence; now he will show how this result can be achieved, and this is an important part of his teaching.

94. About the Four Ways of Obtaining Benevolence

1. Benevolence can be obtained from four quarters: from our person, from our opponents, from the audience, and from the case itself.

94. The Commentator

1. In this section Tullius shows how to win benevolence; since it cannot be obtained but from elements concerning either the people involved or the case, he claims that it can come from four directions: first, from our own person and from that of the people we defend; second, from the persons of our opponents, and from those against whom we speak; third, from the members of the jury, that is, from the people before whom we speak; fourth, from the case and the facts we speak about. These ways will be analyzed exhaustively and in the appropriate sequence.

95. Tullius on the Prologue

1. We can obtain the jury's benevolence from our own person if we speak about our facts and actions without arrogance, and if we dispel all suspicion of guilt or foul dealings; if we dwell upon the evils that have been caused and the difficulties that are still present; if we entreat or plead humbly and submissively.

95. The Commentator

1. To win benevolence from our own person means that we should say, about us and about those on behalf of whom we plead, those things capable of making the audience well disposed toward us. Some concern people, while others concern the case. These will be dealt with exhaustively, since getting acquainted with them will prove extremely interesting and helpful. 2. Tullius points out four ways to obtain benevolence from our person. The first is a soft and polite way to present our facts and our actions without arrogance. By "facts," he means what we do spontaneously and not because we are compelled by law or force. This is how Dido, when speaking of Aeneas, won the benevolence of her audience. She said: "I gave safe shelter in my house to one who was in serious danger after a shipwreck, and even before I heard his name, I gave him my kingdom."[162] In this way she explained how she had been merciful toward Aeneas, who was running away from the destruction of Troy. 3. In fact, we tend naturally, and not because we are forced, to have pity on strangers and to be merciful toward them. On the other hand, we call "duties" what we do because we are compelled, not because it is in our nature. Of both, Tullius says, we should speak mildly and without arrogance. 4. The second way occurs whenever we allay from us and from our people charges and foul suspicions, charges being defined as those crimes we are openly accused of, as it happened to Boethius when he was accused of having written treacherous letters against the emperor, an accusation he was able to reject through one of his main qualities, i.e., his wisdom, when he said: "What can be said about these forged letters? Their forgery would have been clear if we had been present when the accuser gave evidence." 5. "Foul suspicions" are crimes attributed to a certain person, but only in thought, without an open charge, as it occurred when Boethius was believed to adore devils in order to obtain high offices. This he rejected when speaking to Philosophy as follows: "Those who believed that I could have soiled my conscience by committing a sacrilege (or by intercourse with evil spirits) were liars, since You, Philosophy, being firmly in my mind, had dispelled from my soul all desire of mortal things"[163] so that he seemed to imply: "since I had wisdom in myself, I could not possibly have such foul failings." In exactly the same way, Helen, wishing to allay her husband's suspicion from herself, said: "He who trusts me when his life is concerned is suspicious of my beauty, but a brave man should not be afraid of a woman's beauty."[164] 6. The third way occurs whenever we lament the evil we have suffered and the difficulties that are still extant. In this way Boethius, in relating what had

happened to him, won the benevolence of the audience with the following words: "As a reward for my love of truth, I suffered the pains of an unjust charge."[165] Dido, when lamenting her sufferings after Aeneas's departure, obtained the benevolence of her audience by saying: "I am banished. I am going to leave my country, my husband's house and walk strange lands to chase my enemies."[166] In the same way Julius Caesar, once he saw that war was an impending danger, spoke about the evils that could come to him in order to encourage his soldiers to fight, and said: "Bear in mind Caesar's sufferings and look at the chains; think how this head of mine which will be placed on the iron beaks, while my limbs will be broken."[167] 7. The fourth way occurs whenever we humbly entreat or ask for mercy; that is, we devoutly and reverently ask for mercy with great humbleness. An entreaty does not involve any pleading. For example, Pompey, during his mortal battle against Caesar, in order to encourage his soldiers, said: "I leave my last actions and the last years of my life in your hands, since I am not going, in my old age, to submit to anyone, after being used to power in my youth."[168] These requests are at times explicit, as in the case of Pompey, at times implicit, as in the words Dido sent to Aeneas: "I am not saying this because I believe I can persuade you, but since I have lost my honor and the chastity of my body and soul, I can well waste a few unimportant words on a few insignificant things."[169] On the other hand, a plea occurs whenever we plead either in the name of God, for our soul's sake, to obtain something, or in the name of our relatives, as Dido did when she addressed Aeneas, saying: "I plead in the name of your father, of your brothers' powerful weapons, of the companions who left Troy with you, of the gods and of the greatness of Troy," etc.[170] 8. The first sources of benevolence, that is, our person and the people about us, have been discussed. Now the second will be dealt with, that is, the one coming from our opponents and from those against whom we speak.

96. On the Second Prologue

1. This derives from the person of our opponents, if we succeed in bringing hatred, envy, or scorn on them.

96. The Commentator

1. To obtain benevolence at the expense of our opponents, that is, to induce the audience to be well disposed toward us and ill disposed toward our adversaries, is a result that, according to Tullius, can be achieved in

three ways: the first is to ascribe to them qualities that can make them hateful to the audience; the second is to breed envy against them; the third is to make them the object of scorn before the audience. These three ways will be exhaustively discussed.

97. Tullius

1. Hatred will be aroused if our adversaries are said to have acted against nature, with arrogance, cruelty, or malice.

97. The Commentator

1. We can arouse hatred in the audience against our opponents if we claim that they have acted unnaturally, that is, against the law of nature, such as eating human flesh or something to the same effect, which the Commentator is not going to mention at present. The same we obtain if we say that they have acted with arrogance, without fear or consideration of their betters whom they held in poor esteem; or if we claim that they behaved cruelly without pity or mercy toward the lesser people or the poor, the sick, and the miserable; if we say that they acted maliciously, that is, falsely, wickedly, in a way that was disloyal or evil, i.e., unfeasible and against the accepted behavior. 2. Of all this we can find an example in Boethius's words against the emperor Nero: "We know very well how much ruin he caused by setting fire to Rome and murdering his own relatives, his brother and his mother."[171] An equally bad behavior is related by Eurifiles about Medea, who wandered dishevelled among the tombs, picking up the bones of the dead.[172] 3. Now the Commentator has explained how, according to Tullius, we can arouse hatred in the audience and a negative disposition against our opponent. Hence, he will explain how we can arouse their envy.

98. Tullius

1. Envy is aroused by mentioning our opponents' strength, power, wealth, relations, money, unbearable pride, and by emphasizing how they value all these things more than the case they are involved in.

98. The Commentator

1. We can arouse the envy and the anger of the audience against our opponents if we mention the strength of their bodies and of their souls, both

in wartime and in peace; their power, that is, the high offices they obtain, and their dominions; their wealth, that is, the slaves, the servants, the possessions they have, their family connections, their noble birth, their influential relatives, and the number of their followers; their money, both gold and silver. Of all this we shall emphasize the disagreeable evil actions they perpetrate, as well as the unbearable pride and arrogance they show. 2. This is what Sallust said to the Romans: "I know very well that Catiline is of noble descent and is endowed with a great physical and mental strength, but he uses all his power to betray people and ruin states," while Catiline argued against the Romans: "They have honor and power, we are left with dangers and poverty.[173] 3. After discussing how envy can be aroused against our opponents, we are going to show how we can arouse contempt against them.

99. Tullius

1. Contempt will be aroused in the audience against our opponents if we say that they have no art, are slow and lazy, engaged in useless things, and devoted to idle lust.

99. The Commentator

1. We can arouse contempt in the audience against our opponents, that is, we can make the audience despise them and consider them worthless, if we say that they are ignorant, unwise with no object in their lives; lazy, often asleep, or moving about as if they were asleep; slow in everything; engaged in useless things; devoted to idle lust, either because they eat and drink too much or busy themselves with harlots, games, and taverns. 2. After showing how we can obtain the benevolence of our audience at the expense of our opponents, by arousing hatred, envy, and contempt against them, we go back to our main subject and discuss how to obtain benevolence from the persons of the audience, and this is the third aspect.

100. The Audience's Benevolence

1. We can win the benevolence from the persons of our audience by maintaining that they behave with decision, wisdom, meekness in every situation, by emphasizing the great honesty of their beliefs, their authority, and the expectations of people as far as their decisions are concerned.

100. The Commentator

1. We can win the benevolence of the audience by praising their qualities and their actions for their force, loyalty, courage, wisdom, meekness, that is, for a reasonable humbleness, by emphasizing the good opinion people have of them and of their honesty, by intimating how anxiously everybody waits for their decision on the case under scrutiny, how firmly everyone believes that it is going to be so just and authoritative that it will be a model for similar cases in the future. 2. Of one such brave action Tullius commended Caesar: "You have tamed barbarous peoples," he said, "and conquered many countries and rich lands by your strength."[174] 3. And he also praised him for his wisdom in the case of Marcus Marcellus: "When in anger, which is a great enemy of reason, you kept your head."[175] 4. He also praised Caesar for his meekness: "In victory, which naturally nurtures pride, you remained humble," he said. 5. Tullius praised him for his honest disposition: Caesar was not always favorable to Tullius but nonetheless kept him in his service; Tullius was so upset with Caesar's enmity that he was unable to attend to his rhetoric as he used to until Caesar gave him his favor once more. About that Tullius said: "You have given back to me and to my former life all I had been used to and had been taken away from me, but even then you still left me some intimations of hope."[176] This he said because Caesar had kept him in his service, thus not depriving him of his good name. 6. Tullius also praised Caesar when he was expecting a favorable verdict concerning the case of Marcus Marcellus: "The sentence that is expected of you about this case does not concern this one only, but all the cases similar to it, so that your decision will be a model for all the others."[177] 7. After showing how benevolence can be obtained from the persons of the audience, Tullius will show how it can be achieved from facts.

101. Benevolence from Facts

1. This can be obtained if we praise and exalt our case while spitefully disparaging our opponents'.

101. The Commentator

1. We can win the benevolence of the audience from the very facts we are discussing if we describe their circumstances in a way that is favorable to us and unfavorable to our opponents, when we praise our attitude and

make the other part's appear to be of little importance and despicable; this Pompey did when encouraging his followers in the war against Caesar: "Our case is a rightful and just one, so it is worthier than that of our enemies, and we can firmly hope to have God's help."[178] Now the four ways that can win us the audience's benevolence have been discussed, and we can proceed to show how to obtain the attention of the audience.

102. On Obtaining the Attention of the Audience

1. We shall obtain the attention of the audience if we show that what we are speaking about is great, new, or extraordinary and that it is of general interest, or perhaps concerns either those who are listening to it, some illustrious men, the immortal gods, or the main interest of the Commune; if we promise to speak briefly about our case, or submit the point—or the points, if there are more than one—to be decided on.

102. The Commentator

1. After discussing how to win the benevolence of those people before whom we deliver our oration, so that we can make their minds favorable to our case and unfavorable to our opponents', in this section Tullius proposes to show how we can, in the exordium, that is, at the beginning of our speech, obtain the attention of our audience, so that their minds can be made alert to what we have to say. This can be done in various ways, which have been analyzed before. 2. It can certainly be stated that everybody will be attentive and dispose himself to listen if in the exordium I say that I am going to deal with great and important matters, as the intelligent author of Alexander's stories did when he began as follows: "I am going to speak of such great enterprises as the ones performed by the man who conquered the whole world and subjected all nations."[179] 3. The same occurs if I say that I am going to deal with new events and tell what has already happened or is going to happen because of these new facts, as Catiline did when he said: "Since the force of the Commune has come into the hands of the rabble and the mob, we, who are noble and powerful, worthy of honors, have become rabble without honor, favor, or authority."[180] 4. The audience's attention can also be obtained if I claim that I am going to tell unbelievable stories, like the saint who said: "I will speak about that holy woman who conceived and gave birth to a son being a virgin before and after the event,"[181] which is unbelievable, since it appears to be against nature. In the same way, the Greeks used to say: "It is impossible to believe that Paris

could be so foolishly daring as to come to this country and take Helen away."[182] 5. The audience's attention can also be obtained if I claim that the subject I am going to talk about has a general interest or perhaps concerns everyone in the audience, as Cato said when speaking about Catiline's conspiracy: "These noble citizens have conspired to burn and destroy our land, and their leader is at the head of them; so you have to think carefully about what kind of verdict you must pronounce against those very cruel citizens who have been captured within the city walls."[183] 6. Attention will also be obtained if I say that I am going to speak about important men, that is, people of great name and high office, as Pompey did when talking about the civil war: "You must know that the enemy's arms are ready to destroy this high and glorious Senate," he said.[184] 7. I can also win the attention of the audience if I say that my words concern the gods, as Catiline is said to have done after he had conceived such a horrible crime: "He cried that only the gods above could take the people out of his hands."[185] 8. Attention is also obtained if in the exordium I promise to discuss the case briefly and in few words, as the poet did when he was going to tell the story of Troy: "I will briefly tell how Helen was taken only by deceit, and how only by deceit was Troy seized and destroyed."[186] 9. The audience will also be attentive if in my exordium I suggest that the verdict is to be given on one or more points, i.e., the very ones on which I base my oration and demonstrations, as Orestes did when he said: "I shall prove that I was justified in murdering my mother, since Apollo ordered me to do that because she had murdered my father." We can find examples of all the possible ways to catch the attention of the audience in what Tullius said to Caesar in his oration in defense of Marcus Marcellus: "I cannot help mentioning such meekness, such incredible and unusual mercy, such unbelievable and almost divine wisdom."[187] Once Tullius has clearly shown how audiences can be made attentive to the orator's words, he will proceed to show how they can be made compliant.

103. How to Make Audiences Compliant

1. We shall make our audience compliant if we state openly and briefly what the case is about, that is, what the controversy consists of. Certainly, if you wish to make them compliant, you must at the same time make them attentive, as no one can be really compliant unless he has actually been made ready to listen.

103. The Commentator

1. The people before whom I have to speak can be made compliant, that is, receptive to the features of my case, if in the exordium, that is, at the beginning of my oration, I touch upon the case I am going to discuss briefly and openly, clearly stating what it is about and emphasizing the point where the force of the conflict and of the controversy lies. In this way, Sallust made Tullius compliant by saying: "Although I cannot find in you either discretion or equity, I will answer briefly so that, if you had any wish to slander, you should lose it by listening to my reproach."[188] 2. Many other examples could be given to make the audience compliant, as an attentive reader can see from what has been said before. Since two kinds of exordia have been defined, namely, the opening and the insinuation, and what can appropriately be said at the beginning if the audience must be made benevolent, attentive, and compliant has been discussed, the insinuation will now be dealt with in what follows.

104. The Teaching of the Insinuation

1. Now the time has come to discuss how insinuations should be dealt with. *Insinuatio* has to be used when the case is of an inconceivable kind, that is—as we have said before—when the minds of the audience are ill disposed toward us. This mainly occurs for three reasons: the case has something foul in itself; those who have spoken before seem to have persuaded the audience; or perhaps, when it is our turn to speak, the audience are already tired with too much listening. This last situation often upsets the audience's minds in no less degree than the other two.

104. The Commentator

1. The various ways by which we can make the audience attentive, benevolent, and compliant by means of the kind of exordium called the "opening" have been exhaustively illustrated before. Now it is convenient to show how the same results can be obtained by means of the kind of exordium called *insinuatio*. 2. It has been appropriately said before that the *insinuatio* is a kind of prologue where covered and insincere words are spoken. This is why Tullius says that this gilded[189] prologue should be used whenever our case is in some respect a foul and dishonorable one, and it is of the kind we defined inconceivable when discussing the five kinds of cases; namely, the honorable, the inconceivable, the

insignificant, the dubious, and the obscure. 3. The other four can be dealt with by means of the kind of exordium called the "opening," but here, that is, in the inconceivable case, the insinuation had better be used in order to change the audience's disposition and turn into benevolence and good will what appears to have moved them to hatred. It is, therefore, appropriate to establish in how many ways and in what sort of situations our own case can be classified as inconceivable, and then see how we can cope with it in each case. There are three of them. 4. The first occurs whenever the case has something ugly in it because it concerns an evil person or action, since the minds of the audience are aroused against the evil man or the foul action. 5. The second occurs when the orator who has spoken first has persuaded the audience to the extent that what he said has taken possession of their minds, so that they seem to believe it to be true; in this way, if the audience begin to believe what the opponent says and consider it true, then it is hardly possible for them to be induced to believe what the other part says; on the contrary, they tend to estrange themselves and to turn away from it. 6. The third situation is of a different kind, for it often happens that those people before whom we have to present our case and expound our arguments have been listening for a long time to others who have spoken at length before us, as a consequence of which their minds are tired and not inclined to listen to our words; this is a condition that creates a bad disposition in no lesser degree than the other two. So the orator should weigh his words in order to cope with each adverse situation according to Tullius's teachings.

105. About the Foul Case

1. If the case is so foul that it offends, the person who is the source of the offense should be replaced by another who is appreciated; the reason of the offense should be replaced by something inoffensive; therefore, either the person or the cause of the offense should be discarded in favor of something the audience like, so that they withdraw from what they hate and turn to what they love. You should also pretend not to defend what they think is the object of your defense, and only when the audience are mollified can you, little by little, begin your defense and say that those things that anger your opponents seem unworthy of defense even to yourself. When the audience have been softened, you can argue that you have nothing to do with those matters and that you will say nothing against your opponents, nothing at all; in this way, you do not openly slander those who are loved but surreptitiously avert the sympathy of the audience from

them; sometimes you can mention a verdict which was pronounced in a similar case, or perhaps an authority worth listening to, and then show that the two cases are similar, either of greater or smaller importance.

105. The Commentator

1. In this section Tullius says that if the audience are annoyed with us because our case is, or seems to be, a foul one since it concerns evil people or foul actions, we shall have to use insinuation in our speeches so that the person the audience appear to be angry with can be replaced by another whom the audience appreciate and love. In this way, the presence of a person who is loved covers what is unpleasant, appeases the minds of the audience, and removes their anger against the person they thought to be evil; this is what Ajax did in the controversy between himself and Ulysses about the arms that had belonged to Achilles. 2. For although Ajax was a valiant warrior, he was not much loved nor held in great consideration. On the contrary, Ulysses was much loved because of his great wisdom. Therefore, Ajax, wishing to counterbalance this situation, reminded the audience that he was the son of Telamon, who had conquered Troy at the time of brave Hercules, thereby mentioning first, instead of himself, a person who was pleasing and well liked in order to take advantage of that and to have a favorable verdict.[190] 3. When the case is a foul one because of an evil action, we must mention in our oration something good and pleasant, as Catiline did,[191] in trying to find excuses for his conspiracy against Rome, when he mentioned a just action to conceal an evil one and claimed "I have always helped unhappy people in their predicaments."[192]

NOTES

[1] *Rettorica* in Italian, with a double *t*, according to the medieval fashion. According to Tateo, "Rettorica," p. 895, and Artifoni, "I podestà professionali," p. 701, the name was believed to derive from *rector* rather than *rhetor*. The distinction has a special importance in Brunetto Latini's work, since it highlights his idea that the science of rhetoric is at the service of the Commune. A *rhetor/rector* is therefore a man, ideally the *podestà*, who can rule over people by means of a wise and competent use of rhetoric.

[2] The sources of Brunetto Latini's work are analyzed in the introduction. In addition, it should be emphasized that "philosophers" is here used in a wider sense with respect to the modern meaning of the word. The philosophers "strictu sensu" Brunetto often quotes are Boethius (*De consolatione philosophiae* and *De differentiis topicis*) and Cicero (*De officiis*). Plato and Aristotle are to him recognized authorities who held different opinions about rhetoric. Brunetto shows an excellent knowledge of Aristotle and compares the theories of the Greek philosopher with those of other students of rhetoric (e.g., Hermagoras). He also frequently follows "the Philosopher" in his method of analysis.

³ "Latino" is found in the documents much more frequently than the genitive "Latini," especially when Brunetto speaks of himself. The Christian name is also spelled "Burnetto" (e.g., Brunetto Latini, *Tesoretto*, ed. Pozzi, line 70) and, as Holloway, *Twice-Told Tales*, points out, the metathesis Brunetto/Burnetto is also frequent in the official documents that bear his name.

⁴ The difference in the dimensions of the letters between the translated text and Brunetto's comment is beautifully reproduced in Magliabechiano, II, IV, 127 (M1), Florence, Biblioteca Nazionale Centrale, one of the best manuscripts containing *La Rettorica*, but, of course, it is itself the scribe's interpretation of Brunetto's words.

⁵ Brunetto refers to Cicero's *Prologue*. However, the comment that immediately follows seems to provide a second prologue, this time Brunetto's, which has many of the features of the well-known *accessus ad auctores*, especially in the detailed classification of the different aspects of rhetoric. It is interesting to remark that at times Brunetto seems to refer to his comment rather than to Cicero's text, as if he were the author of the whole treatise. See Baldassarri, "'Prologo' e 'Accessus ad auctores,'" p. 109.

⁶ In the Latin text, the word is *res publica*, an expression Brunetto often translates as "Comune." We have here the first example of Brunetto's "modernization" of Cicero: his main interest is political science, and his model is the Florentine Commune, which he compares to Rome, following the well-known medieval ideal of *translatio*—not, however, of the Empire but of the *res publica*. Moreover, he seems to attribute to Cicero's rhetoric some sort of universal value that could prove useful in Florence as it did in Rome.

⁷ *Sponitore* in Italian, that is, one who expounds somebody's ideas. This is consistent with the fact that Brunetto emphasizes that he is no mere translator of Cicero's text but also its interpreter: he explains, provides examples, and fills gaps in the original. His ambition is really to collaborate with Cicero, and his position as a Commentator gives him a fine opportunity in this respect. In fact, the *Commentator*, unlike the *compilator*, works on only one text which he interprets on the basis of his own ideas. Bonaventure (Bonaventura da Bagnoregio), *Commentaria* 12, defines the Commentator as one who "scribit et aliena et sua, sed aliena tamquam principalia, et sua tamquam annexa ad evidentiam" (quoted in Minnis, *Medieval Theory of Authorship*, p. 94). Brunetto, however, goes even further, and a few pages later calls himself the second author of the book, thereby placing his translation and commentary on the same level with Cicero's writing. Whatever we think of this attitude, his commentary is generally different from the usual word-by-word grammatical analysis which was still customary in schools and shows a certain freedom in the organization of the material, in the logic of the exposition, and in the choice of words. See Alessio, "Brunetto Latini e Cicerone," p. 130.

⁸ The "writing of letters" is the *ars dictaminis*, which had become very important in the political and diplomatic relationships the Florentine Commune had established with other cities and nations. Brunetto himself was a well-known *dictator*.

⁹ The distinction between the extrinsic and the intrinsic aspects of rhetoric is in Victorinus, *Explanationum* 170, where he attributes it to Varro. Boethius, in *De differentiis topicis*, col. 1209, also emphasizes the differences between the two kinds of rhetoric.

¹⁰ Boethius, *De differentiis topicis*, cols. 1205–16.

¹¹ The difference is explained by Victorinus, *Explanationum* 156, whose definition is, however, threefold, and includes *sophista*. However, it is interesting to remark that Brunetto says *rector*, while Victorinus has *rhetor*. Evidently Brunetto tends to identify the ruler with the good rhetorician.

[12] The mention of the influence Pier delle Vigne, the famous poet, letter writer, and legal scholar, had on Emperor Frederick II, which is here ironically stressed, may have caught Dante's attention. See Dante Alighieri, *Inferno* 13.58–61.

[13] Victorinus, *Explanationum* 156, is once more the immediate source, but the origin of the definition is Cicero's *De oratore*. Both Victorinus and Brunetto emphasize the fact that public as well as private controversies are the material of the orator.

[14] This list of the aspects of rhetoric that must be taken into account is in the style of the academic prologue. See note 5.

[15] See note 7. It may be useful to add that Brunetto states that he wishes to "complete" Cicero's work by discussing the art of letter writing, to which he is anxious to attribute the same dignity that was usually given to oratory, and which he practiced with the greatest ability on behalf of the Commune of Florence.

[16] The identity of this person is unknown. Various hypotheses have been made. Brunetto quotes the Tosinghi in *Rettorica* 17, and his friend may have been one of this noble and rich Florentine family, namely, Davizzo della Tosa, but no certainty exists. See *Li Livres dou Tresor de Brunetto Latini* 20 and Inglese, "Latini, Brunetto," p. 5. Brunetto calls him his *porto* (harbor), and this fact has led some scholars, such as Maggini (*La "Rettorica" italiana*) to identify him with Matteo della Porta, but *porto* is probably only an allusion both to the help Brunetto received from him and to the fact that he may have given him shelter in his house. Their friendship must have been a long-standing one, since Brunetto also dedicates the *Tresor* to him.

[17] The *Rhetorica ad Herennium* was believed to be the second volume of Cicero's *De inventione* (*Rhetorica secunda*), and it often follows this treatise in the manuscripts. The belief was widespread throughout the Middle Ages. The first scholar to express doubts, as far as the authorship is concerned, was Lorenzo Valla in the fifteenth century. Since then, the work has been attributed to Cornificius, a rhetorician greatly criticized by Quintilian. Modern scholars prefer to consider the *Rhetorica ad Herennium* the work of an unknown author.

[18] In 1260 Brunetto Latini was sent by the Commune of Florence to Alfonso of Castile in order to persuade the king to claim the imperial crown (against Manfred, Frederick II's son). On his way back (probably in Navarre) he heard about the defeat of the Florentines at Monteaperti (September 4) and learned of the banishment that had been ordered against himself and some of his Guelph followers. He stopped in France (Arras, Paris, Montpellier), where he wrote *La rettorica*, *Tresor*, and probably *Tesoretto* and *Favolello*. He returned to Florence in 1265 with Charles of Anjou. See Davidsohn, *Storia di Firenze*, trans. Klein, 2:78, and Inglese, "Latini, Brunetto," p. 5.

[19] See above, note 16.

[20] Brunetto attributes to Boethius a sentence that can be found only in "Excerpta ex Grillii Commento," p. 597.

[21] This greatly simplified version of the attitudes of Plato and Aristotle towards rhetoric can also be found in the "Excerpta ex Grillii Commento," p. 597.

[22] This idea, which by Brunetto's time had become an ethical commonplace, found its way in a modified form, and almost certainly with no direct relation to Latini's work, into Shakespeare's *Julius Caesar* 3.2.77–78, although the mention of Caesar in the following paragraph of Brunetto's text makes the coincidence peculiar.

[23] Brunetto's translation of *res publica* as "Commune" indicates both his interest in the

Florentine political institutions and the idea that Florence had in the contemporary world the same importance that Rome had had in the past: some sort of *translatio rei publicae* which made Florence the Rome of Brunetto's time.

[24] Cicero did not belong to a noble family. He was a *homo novus*, that is, a plebeian who had reached important positions because of his character and abilities.

[25] Lucan, *Bellum civile (Pharsalia)* 1.70–71. Sundby, *Della vita e delle opera di Brunetto Latini*, p. 463, believes that Brunetto may have come across the quotation in *Moralium dogma philosophorum*, a collection of moral precepts variously attributed to William of Conches, Walter of Chatillon, and Alan de Lille but considered anonymous by modern scholars.

[26] "The other poet" refers to Horace; see *Odes* 3.4.65. The line is also to be found in *Moralium dogma philosophorum*; see Sundby, *Della vita e delle opera di Brunetto Latini*, p. 431.

[27] The line is in Horace, *Carmina* 3.4.65 (see note 26 above), but the same idea can be found in Lucan, *Bellum civile* 1.81. Brunetto has probably used both.

[28] Victorinus, *Explanationum* 157.

[29] Cicero's idea of rhetoric as the source of civilization is especially useful to Brunetto's republican ideals. In this passage Brunetto sees the history of mankind *sub specie rhetoricae*. See also Cox, "Ciceronian Rhetoric in Italy," pp. 48–49.

[30] All the definitions can be found in Victorinus, *Explanationum* 158. Brunetto follows his source closely as far as the definitions of "city," "companion," and "friend" are concerned, while he re-elaborates the other two.

[31] The Italian is "E così me lungamente pensante, la ragione. . . ." Brunetto tends to use Latin constructions when he translates from Cicero, while his language is much more colloquial and "modern" when he comments on what he has translated.

[32] The warlike language is of special interest here. On the one hand, war was a common metaphor for the medieval disputations which were held at the universities and where the debate between the *opponens* and the *respondens* was often understood in terms of a battle. See, for example, Dante, *Paradiso* 24.46–51. On the other hand, the metaphor is extremely appropriate since it emphasizes that eloquence was considered to be at the service of the policy of the Commune, for whose welfare the *podestà*-orator had to "fight."

[33] Victorinus, *Explanationum* 163.

[34] Victorinus, *Explanationum* 159.

[35] This digression—and the simile of the wine vessel—can be found in Victorinus, *Explanationum* 161.

[36] Victorinus, *Explanationum* 161. In this important passage, where rhetoric is interpreted as the very source of civilization, Brunetto becomes more analytical and explains Cicero's text word by word, first quoting the one he is going to explain and establishing some sort of extended *catena* gloss. See Cox and Ward, *The Rhetoric of Cicero*, p. 1.

[37] The same "man of great eloquence and wisdom" is mentioned in *Tresor* 3.7–8, where the story of Amphion, son of Zeus and a symbol for culture and civilization, is related to the power that words have of persuading people to forsake brute force and live according to reason.

[38] The sentence is a modification of St. Paul's definition: "Est fides sperandarum substantia rerum" (Hebrews 11:1; see Dante, *Paradiso* 24.64: "Fede è sustanza di cose sperate").

[39] Cicero, *De officiis* 1.23.

[40] St. Paul's theoretical definition of faith and Cicero's social and ethical concern

("Faith is the foundation of justice") are both useful to Brunetto, whose purpose is to establish firm grounds for the relationship between rhetoric and the government of the city-states.

[41] Victorinus, *Explanationum* 167.

[42] "Quality" and "quantity" are two of the Aristotelian categories. When Brunetto's examination of Cicero's text is more analytical, his knowledge of Aristotle becomes evident and reminds us of the kind of education Brunetto Latini had probably received at the University of Bologna.

[43] This definition of envy is not in Victorinus, whom Brunetto follows closely in this part of his commentary; it can be found in Aristotle, *Rhetoric* 2.9 (1368b) and Ovid, *Metamorphoses* 2.178, where envy is personified and said to smile only at other people's sufferings. In the Middle Ages, Gregory the Great (*Moralia in Iob* 5.46.84) describes it in similar words. We have no proof that Brunetto had a direct knowledge of Ovid's or of Gregory's work; he probably found these examples in encyclopedias, such as the *Moralium dogma philosophorum*. Dante seems to follow a similar tradition in *Purgatorio* 13.133–35.

[44] The relationship between the possession of eloquence and *auctoritas* is an important one for the political use of rhetoric. Cicero says "auctoritas," and Brunetto glosses: "They had authority, that is, they were both honored and feared." Authority is not confined to the intellectual qualities of the ruler but extended to his political activity: the *podestà* is honored for his wisdom, but his reaction is feared when laws are disregarded.

[45] In the literary tradition this is what Fortune does when she turns her wheel. The sentence echoes Boethius's complaint at the beginning of his *De consolatione philosophiae* 1.m1.11–20.

[46] Brunetto amplifies Cicero's statement, which follows Aristotle, *Politics* 1.2 (1252a) and, by means of a perfect syllogism, shows that a good rhetorician is the best possible person. This lays the ground for the following argument, which states that rhetoric is part of the science of politics, both being activities typical of human beings, as distinct from those typical of the other animals.

[47] "Genus" and "species" are, of course, part of the Aristotelian classification of the natural world. Brunetto's examples are drawn from the actual life of Florence. The names he mentions, Tosinghi and Davizzo, have led some scholars to make assumptions on the identity of the friend he met in France (see above, note 16).

[48] Brunetto extends the Aristotelian classification in order to show that rhetoric is part of the science of politics, which, in turn, is part of philosophy. He therefore engages in a *regressio ad infinitum*, where he tries to sketch a history of human knowledge that will be fully developed in *Tresor*. This is the part of *La rettorica* that is closest to the medieval encyclopedic ideal.

[49] The closest definition is in Isidore of Seville, *Etymologiae* 2.24.9. Brunetto Latini uses the spellings *phylos* and *sophya*.

[50] Isidore of Seville, *Etymologiae* 2.24.9.

[51] Isidore of Seville, *Etymologiae* 2.25.3.

[52] Brunetto modifies Isidore of Seville, *Etymologiae* 2.24.6; in this way, he creates some confusion, since dialectics appears twice in his classification of sciences. Such classification is, however, much more articulate with respect to the classical division into arts of the Trivium and of the Quadrivium and is the result of the greater knowledge the intellectuals of the fourteenth century had of Aristotle's works. See Grabman, *Storia del metodo scolastico*,

2:45–46; Lafleur, *Quatres introductions à la philosophie*, pp. 129–32; and Beltrami, p. xiii. Brunetto may have known the *Accessus philosophorum VII artium liberalium*, which circulated in France in the 1230s (Lafleur, p. 179ff; Beltrami, p. xiv).

[53] See above, note 52. *Ephidics* (*fidique* in *Tresor*) probably derives from "apodictics" and "epidictics." The word is so unusual that some manuscripts of *Rhetoric* have mistaken it for "Physics." This classification of logic can also be found in a short anonymous treatise contained in Muenich, Bayerische Staatsbibliothek, Clm. 331. See Grabman, *Storia del metodo scolastico*, 2:58–59; Beltrami, p. xiv.

[54] See above, note 52. "Physics" does not correspond to what we mean by this word today. It is rather more similar to "physiology," while the study of the properties of matter was known as "natural philosophy" (*philosophia naturalis*). "Physics" is therefore not a completely correct translation, but since this is the way it is always mentioned in medieval vernacular texts, I prefer not to use words which did not exist at the time Brunetto was devising his classification.

[55] This is the traditional classification of the arts of the Quadrivium.

[56] The same classification can be found in *Tresor* and has been assumed to derive from Eustratius's *Comment on Nicomachean Ethics*. See Marchesi, *L'Etica Nicomachea nella tradizione latina medievale* and *Tresor*, p. xiv.

[57] In this classification politics includes all the public activities that take place within the city-state and where the crafts (by deeds) are considered as important as the intellectual professions (by words).

[58] The usual classification of the arts of the *Trivium* is here seen in a new light, since these arts are considered part of the art of politics.

[59] "Barbarism," i.e., an incorrect use of words, and "solecism," an incorrect construction of a sentence, are considered to include all the possible mistakes in the use of language. See *Rhetorica ad Herennium* 4.12.17.

[60] The distinction between rhetoric *cum lite* (with a lawsuit), or *sine lite* emphasizes the fact that rhetoric can be equally important for the political life of a city even if it does not get into law courts. Letters, official documents, and speeches were of a greater general interest than private litigations. Narrations and fables provided examples of good or bad behavior, and the old stories were a useful pedagogical instrument in schools and universities. See Copeland, *Rhetoric, Hermeneutics and Translation*, pp. 182–84, and Mehtonen, "Poetics, Narration and Imitation," pp. 295–96.

[61] *Artificiosa eloquentia* is one of the expressions the Latin authors employed for the Greek word *rhethoriké*. See Cox and Ward, *The Rhetoric of Cicero*, p. 7.

[62] Boethius, *De differentiis topicis*, col. 1199.

[63] Victorinus, *Explanationum* 171.

[64] Boethius, *De differentiis topicis*, col. 1208.

[65] Gorgias of Lentini (fifth century B.C.) is considered one of the inventors of sophistry and is often, from Plato onward, held responsible for the negative aspects of rhetoric. This may in part explain why Brunetto says that he is less reliable than younger rhetoricians.

[66] Aristotle, *Rhetoric* 1358a.35.

[67] Aristotle, *Rhetoric* 1356b.7.

[68] The original has *anegare*, possibly a misunderstanding of the Latin *necare*. The example can be found in Boethius, *De differentiis topicis*, col. 1177; see Maggini, *La "Rettorica" italiana*, p. 34.

[69] Catiline is *the* enemy of Rome, and Brunetto mentions him whenever he considers

facts or people who threatened the existence of the republic. Catiline is also frequently mentioned in *Tresor*, and Brunetto's main source for his life and enterprises is a book, partly translated from Sallust, called *Li fet des Romains*. See Maggini, *La "Rettorica" italiana*, p. 36, and Beltrami, p. xix.

[70] The Italian has *speciale*, and it means "related to the species" and not to the individual. Hence, the translation "theoretical and general."

[71] Campo Marzio (Campus Martius) was where political assemblies were held. Brunetto emphasizes the ethical aspect of these meetings.

[72] The Italian has "podestà delle genti," and *podestà* is here used in the etymological sense of *potestas*, i.e., political power, but of course the allusion is to the Florentine civic authority.

[73] The allusion is probably to the third Macedonian war (171–68 B.C.), also mentioned in *Tresor*, 3.35.

[74] The example is probably Brunetto's invention and is based on the frequent contrasts between the various city-states. In *Tresor* 3.2.10, Milan and Cremona are replaced by "the king of France and the king of England."

[75] In the second book of his *Nicomachean Ethics* Aristotle deals with the difference between virtue as a deliberate choice and virtuous actions engendered by fear, but the exact sentence Brunetto quotes is nowhere to be found in this treatise. We do not know what text of Aristotle's work Brunetto was using, and the sentence appears to be devised for some collection of moral precepts. See *Tresor*, pp. xvii–xviii.

[76] A direct answer to this question, i.e., whether Julius Caesar was right in conquering France, might have been embarrassing for Brunetto, who lived in France at the time he wrote *La rettorica* and had been received and protected there when banished from Florence.

[77] Hermagoras of Temnos (second century B.C.) is quoted by Sextus Empiricus, Cicero, Quintilian, and Augustine. No treatise of this rhetorician survives; he is said to have devised the theory of the *constitutiones*.

[78] Aristotle, *Rhetoric*, see above note 66.

[79] Aristotle, *Rhetoric*, see above note 66. Cicero and Brunetto seem to think that Hermagoras, in contrast with Aristotle, had a too extensive idea of the field of rhetoric.

[80] The controversies on the *summum bonum* Brunetto quotes are the traditional ones, which Brunetto oversimplifies, as he often does when philosophical questions are at issue. At the time he was writing, however, the question had acquired a new importance owing to the work of the so-called Latin Averroists (Siger of Brabant and Boethius of Dacia, among others), who argued that the intellectual activity can be considered the *summum bonum* in man's life, thus preparing the ground for the appreciation of scientific research as distinct from theological doctrine. Some of their propositions were to be condemned by Bishop Tempier in 1277, but the ideas were by that time well known all over Europe. It has been argued that Guido Cavalcanti and Dante Alighieri (especially in his *Convivio*) follow in part the theories of these Parisian masters. See Corti, *Principi della comunicazione letteraria*, pp. 21–41, and Imbach, *Dante, la philosophie et les laïcs*, pp. 141–49.

[81] At crucial moments of his analysis Brunetto tends to comment on Cicero's text sentence by sentence, as he had certainly learned at the University of Bologna, where he was probably educated. The *lectura* is a method he does not generally follow, as has already been remarked (see above, note 7), but when his discourse is more formal, as in this case, when he is about to introduce the different parts of rhetoric, he tends to deal with them in a more academic way. Cicero may have misunderstood Hermagoras's thought, but it seems that

the Greek rhetorician was trying to extend the field of rhetoric to subjects and questions normally dealt with by philosophers.

[82] Aristotle, *Rhetoric* 1358.7 (see above, note 66), and Victorinus, *Explanationum* 177.

[83] In Latin in Brunetto's text. In English: invention, disposition, style, memory, delivery.

[84] Boethius, *In topica Ciceronis*, col. 1060.

[85] Brunetto's host in France. See above, note 16.

[86] Brunetto extends the example given by Boethius (see above, note 84) to the proceedings of invention and disposition. Geoffrey of Visauf, in his *Poetria nova* 2.43–54, describes the writing of poetry in the same way. Brunetto never quotes Vinsauf, but in *Tresor* 3.13 the theory of *amplificatio* is completely based on *Poetria nova*. See Crespo, "Brunetto Latini e la 'Poetria Nova' di Geoffroi de Vinsauf."

[87] Proverbs 27:6.

[88] The distinction is in *Rhetorica ad Herennium* 3.16, which was believed to be Cicero's. See above, note 17, and Carruthers, "Rhetorical *memoria* in Commentary and Practice," pp. 218–19.

[89] This definition can also be found in *Rhetorica ad Herennium*, 3.16.

[90] A similar passage can be found in Boncompagno da Signa, "Rhetorica Novissima," p. 297.

[91] Literally, *porto* (harbor) in Italian.

[92] *Inventio* is feminine in Latin and in Italian (*invenzione*). In his translation Brunetto uses a metaphor, perhaps misunderstanding Cicero's expression (*princeps*, i.e., "the first"), and calls *inventio* the "princess" of all parts of rhetoric. I follow the possible personification by using the feminine personal pronoun "she".

[93] The *Rhetorica ad Herennium*, usually considered the second of Cicero's rhetorical treatises.

[94] *Porto* (harbor) in Italian, the usual metaphor Brunetto uses when mentioning his friend.

[95] *Constitutio* in Latin. The issue is at the basis of all legal cases, and its parts include all sorts of legal arguments.

[96] Brunetto explains *constitutio* etymologically, since he says that the orator *costituisce*, i.e., establishes and arranges, his arguments concerning the fact.

[97] Brunetto has probably invented this example.

[98] This example can be found in Victorinus, *Explanationum* 181. In giving instances of the different cases an orator may have to face, Brunetto endeavors, for the sake of clarity, to devise situations that provide the rhetorician with clear alternatives.

[99] The example concerns Orestes and was very frequently used to show the complexity of a case an orator may have to discuss.

[100] These examples are probably Brunetto's invention.

[101] The example is given at length in *Rhetorica ad Herennium*, 1.11.18.

[102] Victorinus, *Explanationum* 180.

[103] Victorinus, *Explanationum* 181. Brunetto often uses direct questions in order to make the controversy more evident.

[104] Cato and Cicero had both strongly argued that Catiline and his followers had to be sentenced to death, while Julius Caesar wanted them to be kept in prison but not executed. Therefore, the personalities of Cicero and Cato were often considered together.

[105] Victorinus, *Explanationum* 181.

[106] Catiline's conspiracy had been represented in the speeches of Cato and of Cicero as

an extremely serious danger for Rome. Caesar, who had argued that the conspirators had better be kept in prison but should not be put to death, was often accused of not defending Rome with the necessary energy. Brunetto elaborates on that to prove his case.

[107] The example is probably Brunetto's invention.

[108] The example is Brunetto's invention.

[109] The example is not, as far as I know, in the sources, but it may have had something to do with Brunetto's own situation, for in France the Florentine law was not valid.

[110] This little story, probably invented by Brunetto, is an example of a completely absurd charge.

[111] The example is probably Brunetto's invention.

[112] These examples are also present in *Rhetorica ad Herennium* 4.15.22. See also Victorinus, *Explanationum* 181. Fregellae rebelled against Rome and was destroyed in 125 B.C.

[113] Cf. *Rhetorica ad Herennium* 4.15.22. Brunetto does not make any distinction between mythological tales and historical events. "Eloquent" is conjectural; see Maggini, *La "Rettorica" italiana*, 64.

[114] Whatever the origin of this example, Brunetto chooses two very common names (Robert and Walter) and establishes a lively dialogue between the two in order to emphasize the meaning of the story and make it easily understandable.

[115] The example is probably invented.

[116] See *Rhetorica ad Herennium* 1.11.19, and Victorinus, *Explanationum* 183ff., for an exhaustive discussion. *Causa definitiva* in Cicero's text indicates a controversy that concerns definition. Therefore, "definitive" (*De inventione*, trans. Hubbell) does not seem to be an appropriate translation. *OED* has "definitional": "pertaining to definition."

[117] Brunetto takes the name of a population (Allobroges) for a Christian name. In fact, Volturcius was one of the people arrested for the Catiline conspiracy and gave many details about it. The episode is in Sallust, *De coniuratione Catiline* 42.1.

[118] Brunetto makes his examples more lively by giving his characters a name, as if they were real.

[119] The Latin text has "iure consulti," which Brunetto renders as "savi di ragione" (wise and competent, i.e., legal scholars or law experts).

[120] The Italian text has *disciolta*, which is the literal translation of the Latin *absoluta*. Brunetto's definition is therefore rather tautological.

[121] The example is discussed in detail in Cicero, *De inventione* 2.23.69. The bronze trophy the Thebans erected after defeating the Lacedaemonians was criticized since it appeared to be a constant reminder of the enmity between the two peoples.

[122] The example, which Cicero used for the first time in *De inventione* 1.13.18, became a classic in rhetorical treatises.

[123] Brunetto modifies the story told by Cicero in *De inventione* 2.31.95, where a sacrifice to Diana is mentioned.

[124] People from Cahors were notorious for the practice of usury. Dante (*Inferno* 11.50) mentions Cahors with Sodoma as the two cities that most disregarded God's law, thereby bringing together the biblical story and the facts of his own times. Boccaccio calls all usurers *caorsini*. In *De inventione* 2.31.96–97, Cicero tells a similar story about the Lacedaemonians. Brunetto often modifies the examples in order to emphasize that their meanings apply to modern situations as well.

[125] In *De inventione* 2.32.98 the harbor is that of Rhodes. In changing the place where the episode is supposed to have occurred, Brunetto probably wishes to present facts his readers could feel more familiar with and nearer to their experience.

[126] That is, judges who have taken an oath in court.

[127] The "Consiglio degli Anziani" was composed of the oldest and theoretically the wisest politicians in Florence, just as the Senate had been in ancient Rome.

[128] Brunetto here attributes to the Commune of Florence an episode (ambassadors sent to the pope) which is told in *De inventione* 2.29.87 and concerns the Rhodians who were appointed as ambassadors to Athens.

[129] No source has been found for this episode. Brunetto may have invented it in order to emphasize the well-known enmity that existed between Cato and Catiline.

[130] See above, note 122.

[131] The episode can be found in Sallust, *De coniuratione Catilinae* 26.4ff. Brunetto mentions the "Commune of Rome," which is, of course, historically incorrect, but it shows that this form of government was for him the highest political expression of democracy and freedom.

[132] The translative issue is concerned with questions of procedure and is normally raised by lawyers who tend to prevent the actual trial from beginning by claiming that the issue itself is vitiated.

[133] Brunetto seems to have misunderstood Cicero's Latin (*an eo colonia deducatur*) which means: "whether a colony should be established there." See Maggini, *La "Rettorica" italiana*, 122.

[134] Brunetto repeats here Cicero's example, since it appears to prove the point with great evidence.

[135] In *De inventione* 2.42.123, Cicero does not mention the name of the city, while Brunetto chooses to attribute the episode to Lucca.

[136] In Cicero's *De inventione* 2.49.144, the tyrant is Alexander of Ferae (in Thessaly). Brunetto does not mention his name, perhaps to avoid confusion with Alexander the Great. See Maggini, *La "Rettorica" italiana*, p. 30.

[137] In *De Inventione* 2.40.116, Cicero simply mentions a father who leaves a treasure to his son. Brunetto attributes the episode to Alexander the Great, perhaps because he was traditionally thought to be extremely generous.

[138] This strange episode is probably Brunetto's invention.

[139] *De inventione* 2.51.153–54. Cicero does not mention names or places. Brunetto, however, speaks of a ship which was sailing from Pisa toward Tunis. The commercial relationships between Pisa and Tunis are a historical fact. In 1264 a treaty had been signed between the city of Pisa and the Emirate of Tunis. See Maggini, *La "Rettorica" italiana*, pp. 30–31.

[140] The example is Brunetto's invention. The two names Lodoigo and Anibaldo make the controversy lively. The reader can easily imagine a heated debate between the two.

[141] The usual example (see above note 122). Brunetto tries to make the most of the episodes he mentions, so that they can be seen from various viewpoints. When the argument develops from a well-known episode (Cicero says *pervulgato*, i.e., "widespread"), it is easier for the reader to appreciate the subtlety of a kind of reasoning.

[142] Brunetto elaborates on the well-known example in order to show how a defense can be strengthened by adding detail to detail. See also Victorinus, *Explanationum* 153.

[143] The episode is now examined from the point of view of Clytemnestra.

[144] The quarrel between Ajax and Ulysses for the possession of Achilles's arms is told at length in Ovid, *Metamorphoses* 13, where Ajax is said to have killed himself after the arms had been given to Ulysses. Brunetto's direct knowledge of Ovid has been questioned by some scholars. However, in his other possible source, Benoît de Sainte Maure's *Roman de Troie*, the quarrel between Ajax and Ulysses does not concern Achilles's arms but the Palladium.

[145] Brunetto draws his examples from myth and history as well as from the actual life of the Florentine Commune and from the activities that used to take place there.

[146] *[P]orto* (harbor) in Italian. See above, note 16. It is not completely clear whether Brunetto is speaking about Cicero's work or about his own. The fact that he mentions his host probably indicates that he is speaking in his capacity of "second author."

[147] These activities had all become very important at the time Brunetto worked for the Florentine Commune where he played an important part in them.

[148] Brunetto is not only anxious to give the *ars dictaminis* the same dignity oratory traditionally had but also to interpret it in terms of adversarial rhetoric, since this was important for the diplomatic relationships of the Communes.

[149] The same definition can be found in Guido Faba, "Summa dictaminis," p. 287.

[150] Boethius, *De differentiis topicis*, col. 1207.

[151] Perhaps Brunetto refers to Guido Faba ("Summa dictaminis"), whose opinion he also mentions in *Tresor* 3.71.2.

[152] "Oddofredi" is presumably Odofredus, the well-known legal scholar, who taught at the University of Bologna from 1236 to 1260. Brunetto calls him a "judge," but he was probably mainly a lawyer.

[153] For all these similes, Brunetto follows closely the treatise by Bene da Firenze, *Candelabrum*, composed about 1220. See Maggini, *La "Rettorica" italiana*, p. 58.

[154] Cf. Guido Faba, "Summa dictaminis," p. 43.

[155] Cf. Guido Faba, "Summa dictaminis," p. 42, where the expressions suggested by Brunetto can also be found.

[156] The argument is in Victorinus, *Explanationum* 184. "Genus," "species," "substance," and "accident" are drawn from the Aristotelian language with which Brunetto was familiar.

[157] This is a different version of the episode which has been used many times as an example. See Victorinus, *Explanationum* 196. The mention—here for the first time—of Apollo's order emphasizes the difficulty of the judge's decision.

[158] The example seems to be a general one. However, the lesson *de filio* is uncertain, and it has been suggested that it might conceal a proper name. See Maggini, *La "Rettorica" italiana*, p. 164.

[159] Pompey's exordium can be found in Lucan, *Bellum civile (Pharsalia)* 7.439.

[160] "Sino" is probably Sinon (*Aeneid* 2.57–198). Virgil's lines are greatly modified, but no intermediate source has been found.

[161] Virgil, *Georgics* 4.1–5. There is no certainty that Brunetto knew Virgil directly, but no other source for the episode of the bees has been found.

[162] Ovid, *Heroides* 7.89–90.

[163] Boethius, *De consolatione philosophiae* 1.pr.4.

[164] Ovid, *Heroides* 17.173–74.

[165] Boethius, *De consolatione philosophie* 1.pr.4.

[166] Ovid, *Heroides* 7.115–16.

[167] Lucan, *Bellum civile (Pharsalia)* 7.304–5.

[168] Lucan, *Bellum civile (Pharsalia)* 7.380–82.

[169] Ovid, *Heroides* 7.3–6.

[170] Ovid, *Heroides* 7.157–58. See Maggini, *La "Rettorica" italiana*, p. 44.

[171] Boethius, *De consolatione philosophiae* 2.m.6.

[172] The quotation has long puzzled scholars. "Euriphiles" was originally believed to be a mistake for "Euripides," and the text was corrected by the fourteenth-century editor of *La Rettorica* accordingly. All the manuscripts, however, have "Euriphiles," a name which is never connected to Medea. On the other hand, Euripides never speaks about tombs and bones when describing his Medea. Seneca's Medea appears to have something in common with the way Brunetto introduces her (*Medea* 670–842). In *Metamorphoses*, book 7, Medea is described as an enchantress "humeris infusa capillos" who causes "manesque exire sepulchris": not exactly the same but not far from Brunetto's words. In *Heroides*, however, the lines corresponding to Brunetto's translation are spoken by Hypsypiles, who says of Medea: "Per tumulos errat passis discincta capillis / certaque de tepidis colligit ossa rogis" (7.89–90). Brunetto has probably taken Hypsypiles for an author. See Maggini, *La "Rettorica" italiana*, pp. 51–52.

[173] Sallust, *De coniuratione Catilinae* 20.7.

[174] Cicero, *Pro M. Marcello* 3.8. After Pompey's defeat at Pharsalus, M. Marcellus had refused to submit to Caesar and lived in exile. The Senate asked Caesar to forgive him and allow him to return to Rome, which Caesar granted. The oration, which Brunetto Latini translated, is more a praise of Caesar's benevolence than an actual defense of M. Marcellus.

[175] Cicero, *Pro M. Marcello* 3.9.

[176] Cicero, *Pro M. Marcello* 1.2.

[177] Cicero, *Pro M. Marcello* 1.4.

[178] Lucan, *Bellum civile (Pharsalia)* 7.349. See Maggini, *La "Rettorica" italiana*, p. 41. The line is re-elaborated by Brunetto.

[179] The source is uncertain. Maggini, in *La "Rettorica" italiana*, p. 51, quotes the *Histoire d'Alexandre* by Lambert Li Tort and Alexandre de Bernai.

[180] Sallust, *De coniuratine Catilinae* 20.8.

[181] The saint is Matthew. See Matthew 1:18.

[182] The episode was, of course, very well known.

[183] Sallust, *De coniuratione Catilinae* 52.1. Brunetto has probably invented the form of the statement.

[184] The exact sentence is not in Lucan, although the concept is often repeated by him.

[185] Sallust, *De coniuratione Catilinae* 20.6.

[186] Brunetto probably invents a quotation for a very well-known episode.

[187] Cicero, *Pro M. Marcello* 1.1.

[188] This is part of an invented invective against Cicero, which was believed to have been pronounced by Sallust. It was an example given in schools and universities, but it was often believed to reproduce a true debate. See Maggini, *La "Rettorica" italiana*, p. 49. The Latin reads: "Cum in te neque modum, neque modestiam ullam animadverto, respondebo tibi, ut si quamvis maledicendo voluptatem cepisti, cum malo audiendo amittas" ("Invectiva in Ciceronem"). Brunetto mistakes *voluptatem* (pleasure) for *voluntatem* (will).

[189] *Indaurato* in the Italian texts, i.e., "gilded over." I keep the metaphorical expression in my translation, since the adjective "gilded" must have had a tradition of that kind in

English as well, if Shakespeare's "gilded butterflies" (*King Lear* 5.3.8–19), more than three centuries later, could be interpreted as a metaphor for flattering courtiers.

[190] Ovid, *Metamorphoses* 13.20 ff.

[191] Sallust, *De coniuratione Catilinae* 35.3.

[192] Here Brunetto's translation stops. We do not know why he did not finish it, after promising a thorough analysis of Cicero's work. He may have become more interested in the writing of an encyclopedia, which included rhetoric as only part of human knowledge. This was *Tresor*, where a greatly revised version of rhetoric can be found in the third book.

Bibliography

Manuscripts

Florence, Biblioteca Medicea Laurenziana, Redi 23.
Florence, Biblioteca Nazionale Centrale, Magliabechiano, II, II, 48.
Florence, Biblioteca Nazionale Centrale, Magliabechiano, II, II, 91.
Florence, Biblioteca Nazionale Centrale, Magliabechiano, II, IV, 73.
Florence, Biblioteca Nazionale Centrale, Magliabechiano, II, IV, 124.
Florence, Biblioteca Nazionale Centrale, Magliabechiano, II, IV, 127.
Florence, Biblioteca Nazionale Centrale, Magliabechiano, II, VIII, 32.
Florence, Biblioteca Nazionale Centrale, Laurenziano, XLIII, 19.
Munich, Bayerische Staatbibliothek, Cod. 1038 (formerly Cod. It. 148).
Oxford, Bodleian Library, MS Canon. Class. Lat. 201.
Vatican City, Biblioteca Apostolica Vaticana, MS Latino 3973.

Primary Sources

Adalbert of Samaria. *Praecepta dictaminum.* Edited by Franz-Josef Schmale. Monumenta Germaniae Historica: Quellen zur Geistesgeschichte des Mittelalters 3. Weimar: Böhlaus, 1961.

Albertano da Brescia. *Liber de doctrina dicendi et tacendi: la parola del cittadino nell'Italia del duecento.* Edited by Paola Navone. Florence: Edizioni del Galluzzo, 1998.

Alighieri, Dante. *Commedia.* Edited by Anna Maria Chiavacci Leonardi. Milan: Mondadori, 1991.

———. *Convivio.* Edited by Cesare Vasoli and Domenico De Robertis. Milan: Ricciardi, 1988.

———. *De vulgari eloquentia.* Edited by Pier Vincenzo Mengaldo, pp. 1–237. Milan: Ricciardi, 1979.

Aristotle. *Etica Nicomachea.* Edited by Carlo Natali. Bari: Laterza, 1999.

———. *Politica.* Edited by Renato Laurenti. Bari: Laterza, 2007.

———. *Retorica.* Edited by Armando Plebe. Bari: Laterza, 1973.

Bartolomeo da San Concordio. *Gli ammaestramenti degli antichi.* Edited by Vincenzo Nannucci. Florence: Ricordi, 1840.

Bene da Firenze. *Bene Florentini Candelabrum.* Edited by Gian Carlo Alessio. Padua: Antenore, 1983.

Biblia sacra iuxta vulgatam versionem. Edited by Robert Weber with Bonifatius Fischer, H. I. Frede, Johannes Gribomont, H. F. D. Sparks, and W. Thiele. 3rd ed. Stuttgart: Deutsche Bibelgesellschaft, 1983.

Boethius. *Boethius' "In Ciceronis Topica."* Translated by Eleonore Stump. Ithaca: Cornell University Press, 1988.

———. *De consolatione philosophae.* Edited by Claudio Moreschini. Turin: UTET, 1994.

———. *De differentiis topicis.* PL 64: 1174–1218.

———. *In topica Ciceronis.* PL 64: 1039–1174.

Bonaventure (Bonaventura da Bagnoregio). *Commentaria in IV libros sententiarum Magistri Petri Lombardi*, vol. 1 of *Opera theologica selecta.* Edited by Leonardo M. Bello. Florence: Ad Claras Aquas, 1934.

Boncompagno da Signa. *Amicitia.* Edited by Sarina Nathan. Rome: Società Filologica Romana, 1909.

———. "Quinque tabulae salutationum." Edited by Steven M. Wight in *Medieval Diplomatic and the Ars dictandi: Editions and Translations.* Scrineum: Saggi e materiali on-line di scienze del documento e del libro medievale, 1999.

———. "Rhetorica Novissima." Edited by Augusto Gaudenzi in *Bibliotheca iuridica Medii Aevi*, 1: 249–97. Bologna: Ex aedibus Angeli Gandolphi typis Societatis Azzoguidianae, 1892.

Cicero, Marcus Tullius. *De inventione.* Translated by Harry M. Hubbell. Loeb Classical Library. Cambridge, MA: Harvard University Press, 1949.

———. *De officiis.* Translated by Walter Miller. Loeb Classical Library. Cambridge, MA: Harvard University Press, 1975.

———. *De oratore.* Translated by Edward William Sutton and Harry Rackman. Loeb Classical Library. Cambridge, MA: Harvard University Press, 1935.

———. *Orazioni cesariane.* Edited by Fabio Gasti. Milan: Rizzoli, 1997.

Compagni, Dino. *Cronica.* Edited by Gino Luzzatto. Turin: Einaudi, 1968.

Dietaiuti, Bondie. "Amor, quando mi membra." In *Antologia della poesia italiana: Il Duecento*, edited by Cesare Segre and Carlo Ossola, pp. 138–41. Turin: Einaudi, 1999.

"Excerpta ex Grillii Commento in primum Ciceronis librum *De Inventione.*" In *RLM*, pp. 596–606.

Faba, Guido. "Summa dictaminis." Edited by Augusto Gaudenzi. *Il Propugnatore* n.s. 3, no. 1 (1890): 287–338, 345–93.

Li Fet des Romains. Edited by Louis Ferdinand Flutre and Kornelis Sneyders de Vogel. 2 vols. Paris: Droz, 1937–38.

Geoffrey of Vinsauf. "Poetria nova." Edited by Edmond Faral in *Les arts poétiques du XIIème et du XIIIème siècle.* Paris: Champion, 1924; repr., Geneva: Slatkine, 1982.

Giamboni, Bono. *Fiore di Rettorica*. Edited by Gian Battista Speroni. Pavia: Dipartimento di Scienza della Letteratura e dell'Arte medioevale e moderna, 1994.

Gregory the Great. *Moralia in Job*. PL 75: 499–76: 782.

Horace, Quintus Flaccus. *The Odes and Epodes*. Translated by Charles E. Bennett. Rev. ed. Loeb Classical Library. Cambridge, MA: Harvard University Press, 1968.

———. *Satires, Epistles and Ars poetica*. Translated by H. Rushton Fairclough. Loeb Classical Library. Cambridge, MA: Harvard University Press, 1926.

Isidore of Seville. *Etymologiarum sive originum libri XX*. Edited by Wallace Martin Lindsay. 2 vols. Oxford: Clarendon Press, 1911, repr., 1987.

Latini, Brunetto. *Favolello*. Edited by Giovanni Pozzi in *Poeti del Duecento*, edited by Gianfranco Contini, pp. 278–84. Milan: Ricciardi, 1960.

———. *Li Livres dou Tresor de Brunetto Latini*. Edited by Francis J. Carmody. Berkeley: University of California Press, 1948.

———. *La Rettorica*. Edited by Francesco Maggini. Preface by Cesare Segre. Florence: Le Monnier, 1915, 1968.

———. "S'eo son distretto inamoratamente." Edited by Cesare Segre and Carlo Ossola, in *Antologia della poesia italiana: Duecento*, pp. 135–37. 2nd ed. Turin: Einaudi, 1999.

———. *Tesoretto*. Edited by Giovanni Pozzi in *Poeti del Duecento*, edited by Gianfranco Contini, pp. 175–277. Milan: Ricciardi, 1960.

———. *Il Tesoretto (The Little Treasure)*. Edited and translated by Julia Bolton Holloway. New York: Garland, 1981.

———. *Le tre Orazioni di Marco Tullio Cicerone dette dinanzi a Cesare per M. Marcello, Q. Ligario e il re Deiotaro, volgarizzate da Brunetto Latini*. Edited by Luigi Maria Rezzi. Milan: Fanfani, 1832.

———. *Tresor*. Edited by Pietro G. Beltrami. Turin: Einaudi, 2007.

Il Libro di Monteaperti. Edited by Cesare Paoli. Florence: Gian Pietro Viesseux, 1889.

Lucan, Quintus A. *Bellum civile (Pharsalia)*. Edited by Renato Badalì. Turin: UTET, 1988.

Moralium dogma philosophorum. Edited by Thor Sundby in *Della vita e delle opere di Brunetto Latini*, pp. 391–509. Florence: Le Monnier, 1884.

Oculus pastoralis. Edited by Dora Franceschi. *Atti dell'Accademia delle scienze di Torino. Classe di scienze morali, storiche e filologiche*, 4th ser., 11 (1966): 1–74.

Ovid. *Heroides*. Edited by Emanuela Salvadori. Milan: Garzanti, 2006.

———. *Metamorphoseon libri*. Edited by Ferruccio Bernini. Bologna: Zanichelli, 1959.

La prosa del Duecento. Edited by Cesare Segre and Mario Marti. Milan: Ricciardi, 1974.

Rhetorica ad Herennium. Edited by Harry Caplan. Loeb Classical Library. Cambridge, MA: Harvard University Press, 1981.

Sallust. *De coniuratione Catilinae.* Edited by Alfred Ernout. Paris: Les Belles Lettres, 1962.

————. "Invectiva in Ciceronem." In *Sallust,* edited by John Carew Rolfe, pp. 492–500. Loeb Classical Library. Cambridge, MA: Harvard University Press, 1931.

Shakespeare, William. *Julius Caesar.* Edited by David Daniell. The Arden Shakespeare. Walton-on-Thames, Surrey: Thomas Nelson, 1998.

————. *King Lear.* Edited by Kenneth Muir. The Arden Shakespeare. London: Methuen, 1969.

Thierry of Chartres. *The Latin Rhetorical Commentaries by Thierry of Chartres.* Edited by Karin M. Fredborg. Toronto: PIMS Studies and Texts, 1988.

Victorinus, Quintus, F. L. "Explanationum in Rhetoricam M. Tullii Ciceronis libri duo." In *RLM,* pp. 153–304.

Villani, Giovanni. *Nuova Cronica.* Edited by Giovanni Porta. 3 vols. Parma: Ugo Guanda, 1990–91.

Virgil. *P. Vergili Maronis Opera.* Edited by Roger Aubrey Baskerville Mynors. London: Oxford University Press, 1969.

Criticism and Scholarship

Alessio, Gian Carlo. "Brunetto Latini e Cicerone (e i dettatori)." *Italia medievale e umanistica* 22 (1979): 123–69.

Armour, Peter. "Brunetto, the Stoic Pessimist." *Dante Studies* 112 (1994): 1–31.

Artifoni, Enrico. "I podestà professionali e la fondazione retorica della politica comunale." *Quaderni storici* 63 (1986): 687–719.

————. "Sull'eloquenza politica del Duecento italiano." *Quaderni medievali* 35 (June 1993): 57–78.

Avalle, d'Arco Sivio. *Ai luoghi di delizia pieni: Saggio sulla lirica italiana del XIII secolo.* Milan: Ricciardi, 1977.

Baldassarri, Guido. "Ancora sulle 'fonti' della 'Rettorica': Brunetto Latini e Teodorico di Chartres." *Studi e problemi di critica testuale* 19 (1979): 41–69.

————. "'Prologo' e 'Accessus ad auctores' nella 'Rettorica' di Brunetto Latini." *Studi e problemi di critica testuale* 12 (1976): 102–11.

Bartuschat, Johannes. "La 'Rettorica' di Brunetto Latini: rhétorique, éthique et politique à Florence dans la deuxième moitié du XIIIe siècle." *Arzanà* 8 (2002): 33–59.

Beltrami, Pietro G. "Tre schede su 'Tresor.'" *Annali della Scuola Normale Superiore di Pisa,* 3rd ser., 23, no. 1 (1993): 115–90.

Boswell, John E. "Dante and the Sodomites." *Dante Studies* 112 (1994): 63–76.

Cammarosano, Paolo. "L'éloquence laïque dans l'Italie communale (fin du XIIe–XIVe siècle)." *Bibliothèque de l'école de Chartres* 158 (2000): 431–42.

Carruthers, Mary. "Rhetorical *memoria* in Commentary and Practice." In *The Rhetoric of Cicero and Its Medieval and Renaissance Commentary Tradition*, edited by Virginia Cox and John O. Ward, pp. 209–37.

Ceva, Bianca. *Brunetto Latini: L'uomo e l'opera*. Milan: Ricciardi, 1965.

Copeland, Rita. "The Ciceronian Rhetorical Tradition and Medieval Literary Theory." In *The Rhetoric of Cicero and Its Medieval and Renaissance Commentary Tradition*, edited by Virginia Cox and John O. Ward, pp. 239–65.

———. *Rhetoric, Hermeneutics and Translation in the Middle Ages*. Cambridge: Cambridge University Press, 1995.

———. "Translation." In *Medieval France: An Encyclopedia*, edited by William A. Kibler and Grover Zinn, pp. 920–23. New York: Garland, 1995.

Copeland, Rita, and Ineke Sluiter, eds. *Medieval Grammar and Rhetoric: Language Arts and Literary Theory, AD 300–1475*. Oxford: Oxford University Press, 2012.

Corti, Maria. *Principi della comunicazione letteraria: introduzione alla semiotica della letteratura*. Milan: Bompiani, 1985.

Cox, Virginia. "Ciceronian Rhetoric in Italy, 1260–1350." *Rhetorica* 17 (Summer 1999): 39–86.

———. "Ciceronian Rhetoric in Late Medieval Italy: The Latin and Vernacular Tradition." In *The Rhetoric of Cicero and Its Medieval and Renaissance Commentary Tradition*, edited by Virginia Cox and John O. Ward, pp. 109–43.

Cox, Virginia, and John O. Ward, eds. *The Rhetoric of Cicero and Its Medieval and Renaissance Commentary Tradition*. Leiden: Brill, 2006.

Crespo, Roberto. "Brunetto Latini e la 'Poetria Nova' di Geoffroi de Vinsauf." *Lettere Italiane* 24 (1971): 97–99.

Curtius, Ernst Robert. *European Literature and the Latin Middle Ages*. Translated by Willard R. Trask. Princeton: Princeton University Press, 1973.

Davidsohn, Robert. *Storia di Firenze*. Trans. G. B. Klein. 5 vols. Florence: Sansoni, 1956.

Davis, Charles T. "Brunetto Latini and Dante." *Studi medievali*, 3rd ser., 8 (1967): 421–50.

Dionisotti, Carlo. *Geografia e storia della letteratura italiana*. Turin, Einaudi, 1999.

Donati, Fortunato. "Lettere politiche del secolo XIII sulla guerra del 1260 tra Siena e Firenze." *Bullettino Senese di Storia Patria* 3 (1896): 222–32; 4 (1897): 101–6; 5 (1898): 257–69.

Folena, Gianfranco *Volgarizzare e tradurre*. Turin: Einaudi, 1991.

Gaeta, Franco. "Dal comune alla corte rinascimentale." In *Letteratura italiana. Il letterato e le istituzioni*, 149–255. Turin: Einaudi, 1982.

Grabman, Martin. *Storia del metodo scolastico*. 2 vols. Florence: La Nuova Italia, 1980.

Hollander, Robert. "Dante's Harmonious Homosexuals (*Inferno* 16.7–90)." 27 June 1996. Accessed April 22, 2015. http://www.princeton.edu/~dante/ebdsa/rh.html.

Holloway, Julia Bolton. *Brunetto Latini: An Analytic Bibliography*. London: Grant and Cutler, 1986.

———. *Twice-Told Tales: Brunetto Latino and Dante Alighieri*. New York: Peter Lang, 1993.

Hunt, R. W. "The Introductions to the *Artes* in the Twelfth Century." *Studia mediaevalia in honorem admodum Reverendi Patris Raymundi Josephi Martin, Ordinis Praedicatorum s. theologiae magistri LXXum natalem diem agentis*, pp. 85–112. Bruges: De Tempel, 1948.

Imbach, Ruedi. *Dante, la philosophie et les laïcs*. Fribourg: Éditions universitaires, 1996.

Inglese, Giorgio. "Latini, Brunetto." In *Dizionario Biografico degli Italiani*, 64:4–12. Rome: Istituto dell'Enciclopedia Italiana, 2005.

———. "Latini, Brunetto." In *Letteratura italiana, diretta da A. Asor Rosa, Gli autori. Dizionario bio-bibliografico e indici*, 2:1036–37. Turin: Einaudi, 1990–91.

Jauss, Hans Robert. "Brunetto Latini als allegorischer Dichter." In *Alterität und Modernität der mittelalterlichen Literatur*, pp. 239–84. Munich: Fink, 1977.

Lafleur, Claude. *Quatres Introductions à la philosophie au XIIIe siècle*. Montréal: Vrin, 1988.

Maffia Scariati, Irene. *A scuola con ser Brunetto. La ricezione di Brunetto Latini dal Medioevo al Rinascimento*. Florence: Edizioni del Galluzzo, 2008.

Maggini, Francesco. *I primi volgarizzamenti dei classici latini*. Florence: F. Le Monnier, 1952.

———. *La "Rettorica" italiana di Brunetto Latini*. Florence: Tipografia Galletti e Cocci, 1912.

Marchesi, Concetto. *L'Etica Nicomachea nella tradizione latina medievale: Documenti ed appunti*. Messina: Trimarchi, 1904.

Mazzoni, Francesco. "Latini, Brunetto." *Enciclopedia dantesca*, 3:579–88. Rome: Istituto dell'Enciclopedia Italiana, 1970.

Mazzotta, Giuseppe. *Dante, Poet of the Desert*. Princeton: Princeton University Press, 1979.

Mehtonen, Paeivi. "Poetics, Narration and Imitation: Rhetoric as *ars aplicabilis*." In *The Rhetoric of Cicero and Its Medieval and Renaissance Commentary Tradition*, edited by Virginia Cox and John O. Ward, pp. 289–312.

Milner, Stephen J. "Communication, Consensus and Conflict: Rhetorical Precepts, the *Ars Concionandi*, and Social Ordering in Late-Medieval Italy." In *The Rhetoric of Cicero and Its Medieval and Renaissance Commentary Tradition*, edited by Virginia Cox and John O. Ward, pp. 365–401.

Minnis, Alastair *Medieval Theory of Authorship*. London: Scolar Press, 1984.

Murphy, James J. "John Gower's 'Confessio Amantis' and the First Discussion of Rhetoric in the English Language." *Philological Quarterly* 41 (1962): 401–11.

————. *Rhetoric in the Middle Ages: A History of Rhetorical Theory from Saint Augustine to the Renaissance*. Berkeley: University of California Press, 1974.

Najemy, John M. "Brunetto Latini's 'Politica.'" *Dante Studies* 112 (1994): 33–51.

Ottokar, Nicholas. *Il Comune di Firenze alla fine del Dugento*. Turin: Einaudi, 1962.

Quain, Edwin A. "The Mediaeval *Accessus ad auctores*." *Traditio* 3 (1945): 215–64.

Rossi, Luciano. "Observations sur l'origine et la signification du mot 'flabel.'" *Romania* 117 (1999): 342–62.

Segre, Cesare. *Lingua, stile e società*. Milan: Feltrinelli, 1963, 1976.

Sgrilli, Paola. "Retorica e società: tensioni anticlassiche nella 'Rettorica' di Brunetto Latini." *Medioevo romanzo* 3 (1976): 380–93.

Sundby, Thor. *Della vita e delle opera di Brunetto Latini*. Trans. R. Renier. Florence: Le Monnier, 1884.

Tabasso, Anna Paola. "Brunetto Latini: la retorica per il governo della città all'uso di Italia." *Portales* 3–4 (2003–4): 30–35.

Tateo, Francesco. "Rettorica." *Enciclopedia dantesca*, 4:895–98. Rome: Istituto dell'Enciclopedia Italiana, 1970.

Istituto Opera del Vocabolario Italiano: Consiglio Nazionale delle Richerche. Accessed April, 2015. www.vocabolario.org.

Ward, John O. "The Medieval and Early Renaissance Study of Cicero's *De inventione* and the *Rhetorica ad Herennium*: Commentaries and Contexts; Appendix. *Catena* Glosses on the *De inventione* of Cicero and the Pseudo-Ciceronian *Rhetorica ad Herennium* from the Eleventh and Twelfth Centuries." In *The Rhetoric of Cicero and Its Medieval and Renaissance Commentary Tradition*, edited by Virginia Cox and John O. Ward, 3–75.

————. "Rhetorical Theory and the Rise and Decline of *Dictamen* in the Middle Ages." *Rhetorica* 19 (2001): 175–23.

Witt, Ronald G. "Brunetto Latini and the Italian Tradition of Ars Dictaminis." *Stanford Italian Review* 3 (1983): 5–24.

————. "Latini, Lovato and the Revival of Antiquity." *Dante Studies*, 112 (1994): 53–61.

Index

(The words *Tullius* and *The Commentator* within Brunetto's text are not indexed)

Typeset in 11/13 Adobe Garamond Pro

Medieval Institute Publications
College of Arts and Sciences
Western Michigan University
1903 W. Michigan Avenue
Kalamazoo, MI 49008-5432
http:/ /www.wmich.edu/medievalpublications

 WESTERN MICHIGAN UNIVERSITY